Lived Experience Phenomenon
Teaching Methods Book 2: LEP Memory Hack Tool

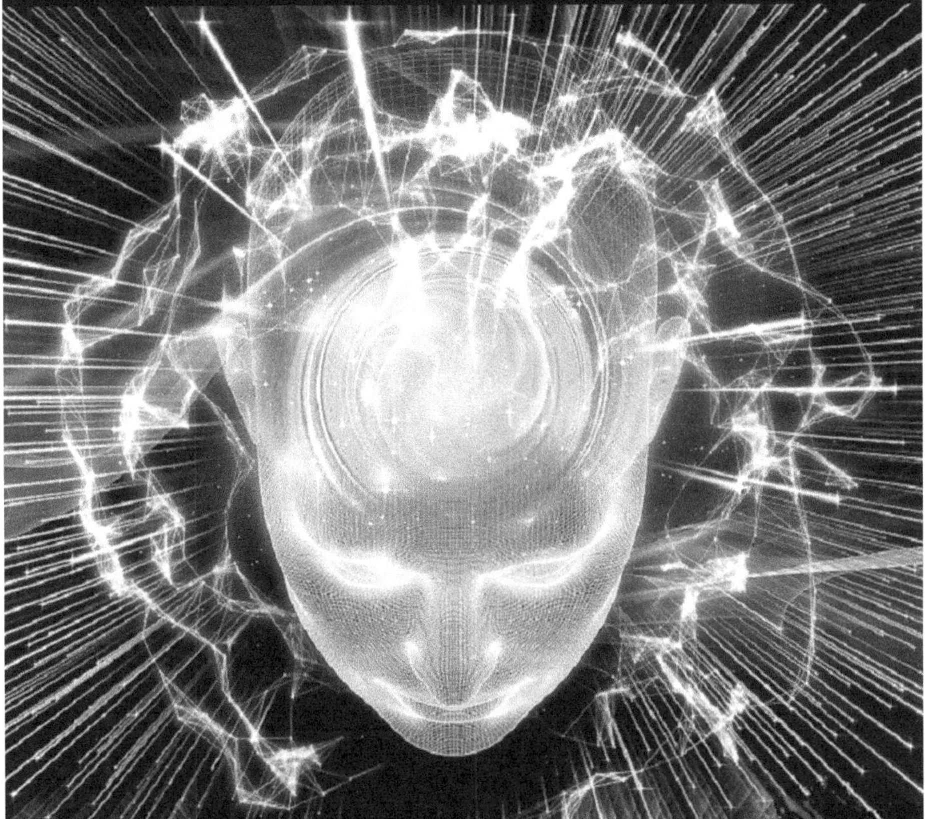

Ana Harvey

Kendall Hunt
publishing company

Cover © Shutterstock, Inc. All interior images courtesy of the author.

Kendall Hunt
publishing company

www.kendallhunt.com
Send all inquiries to:
4050 Westmark Drive
Dubuque, IA 52004-1840

Copyright © 2018 by Kendall Hunt Publishing Company

ISBN: 978-1-5249-7283-7

All rights reserved. No part of this publication may be reproduced, stored in a retrieval system, or transmitted, in any form or by any means, electronic, mechanical, photocopying, recording, or otherwise, without the prior written permission of the copyright owner.

Published in the United States of America

CONTENTS

CHAPTER 1 – THE BIG PICTURE   1

LEP Defined   3
LEP and Inquisitive Reflection   6
Textual and Structural Framing   9
    Textual Framing   10
    Structural Framing   11
LEP Memory Hack Tool   13

CHAPTER 2 – SETTING THE LEP LEARNING TONE   17

Setting the LEP Tone in the Classroom and Online   17
Mind Shift from Content Absorption to Content Connection   24
LEP Mind Mapping   30

CHAPTER 3 – MEMORY SYSTEMS   35

Infusing LEP in the College Classroom Through Memory Systems   36
The Three Memory Systems of Lived Experiences   37
    LEP and Sensory Memory   38
    LEP and Short-Term Memory   41
    LEP and Long-Term Memory   41
        Explicit Memories   42
        Implicit Memories   44
        Procedural Memories   44
    Priming   45
    Framing   46

CHAPTER 4 – LEP MEMORY TRIGGER CATEGORIES   51

LEP Sensory Memory Trigger Categories   53
Categorizing Triggers by Senses   56
- See/Visual   56
- Smell   59
- Taste   60
- Hear   62
- Touch   63

CHAPTER 5 – LEP ATTRIBUTES MEMORY TRIGGER CATEGORIES   67

Categorizing LEP Memory Triggers by Innate Attributes   68
- Linguistic Attribute   69
- Logical Attribute   69
- Musical Attribute   70
- Interpersonal Attribute   71
- Intrapersonal Attribute   72
- Naturalist Attribute   73
- Existential Attribute   74
- Spiritual Attribute   75

Conditioned Response   76
Using LEP Memory Trigger Attributes in Combination   78

CHAPTER 6 – LEP CONTEXT MEMORY TRIGGERS   83

Categorizing LEP Memory Triggers by Contexts   84
Physical Context Triggers   86
Emotional Context Triggers   88
Mental Context Triggers   90
Environmental Context Triggers   92
Personal Belief Context Triggers   94
Moral Context Triggers   96

CHAPTER 7 – LEP MEMORY HACKS   99

Creating Lep Memory Hacks Using Trigger Categories   99
    Creating LEP Memory Hacks Using Sensory Triggers   101
    Creating LEP Memory Hacks Using Attribute Triggers   101
    Creating Memory Hacks Using LEP Trigger Contexts   105

CHAPTER 8 – LEP PERSONAL MEMORY DESIGN PATTERNS   111

Organizing Information Visually Through Organizational Design Patterns   112
    Chronological Design Pattern of Organization   113
    Sequence Design Pattern of Organization   114
    Cause-and-Effect Design Pattern of Organization   116
    Problem-and-Solution Design Pattern of Organization   116
    Compare-and-Contrast Design Pattern of Organization   119

CHAPTER 9 – IT'S PERSONAL: REFRAMING EDUCATION THROUGH LEP TEACHING METHODS   123

Exploring The Possibilities   123
Building the Next Generation of Lep Educational Leaders   126

CHAPTER 10 – LEP CLASS SUPPLEMENTS AND RESOURCES   129

Mind Preparation   129
    Activity 1   *Creative Visualization and Imagery*   131
    Activity 2   *LEP Inquisitive Reflection Activity*   133
    Activity 3   *Quick Inquisitive Reflection—Practice Sheet*   134
    Activity 4   *Content Absorption to Content Connection*   135
    Activity 5   *LEP Textual and Structural Mapping Practice Sheet*   136
    Activity 6   *Understanding the LEP Framing Process*   137
        Understanding the Four Steps of LEP Framing   138

Activity 7   Concept Framing Worksheet 139
Student Activity 8a   Framing with Sensory Memory Triggers   140
Activity 8b   Visual Example of Creating Sensory Triggers
        and Hacks   141
Activity 9   Overview of LEP Memory Trigger Categories   142
Activity 10   LEP Triggers Attribute Practice Worksheet   143
Activity 11   LEP Context Tree Visual Activity for Inquisitive
        Reflection   144
Activity 12   Create Memory Hack   145
Activity 13   Using Imagination Instead of Memories   146
Activity 14   Chronological Pattern of Organization   147
Activity 15   Sequence Pattern of Organization   148
Activity 16   Cause-and-Effect Design Pattern   149
Activity 17   Problem-and-Solution Design Pattern   150
Activity 18   Compare-and-Contrast Design Pattern   151
Lep Educator Preparation Checklist   152

References   155

CHAPTER ONE

THE BIG PICTURE

LEP (LIVED EXPERIENCE PHENOMENON): IT'S PERSONAL
LEP DEFINED
LEP AND INQUISITIVE REFLECTION
LEP TEXTUAL AND STRUCTURAL FRAMING
LEP MEMORY HACK TOOL

LEP Learning and Memory Process

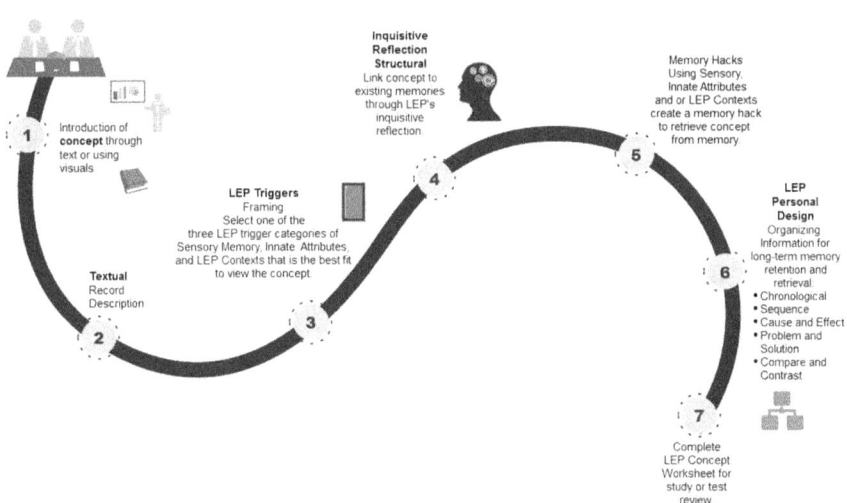

Memories, true or not, "or whether time has rewritten every line," are all a part of the memory tapestry of each person's life gained through the lived experience phenomenon (LEP) that when accessed become valuable tools for learning and long-term memory retention of information. Memory is that which has accrued from former speech, thought, action, behavior, or deed that has created an experience and has been registered in the person's long-term memory. The meaning that is assigned to each memory as it is accrued becomes a tool for new learning and a resource for long-term memory retention because of its ability to expand knowledge and form new meaning and purpose through its applications.

Meaning and purpose are the foundation of LEP teaching and learning because LEP seamlessly moves information from content absorption (meaning) to content connection (personal application and purpose) through the process of LEP's inquisitive reflection. Additionally, LEP's uniquely textual and structural comprehension and long-term memory techniques assure that the information learned is retained long term and ready to be retrieved through LEP's memory hacks when needed. Moreover, one of LEP's key features is that it can be used in combination with any teaching style or independently. LEP also takes advantage of visual information organizational design patterns which aid students in being creative in how they organize the information and take notes. LEP organizational methods assist students to structure and illustrate the concepts in clear visual ways for easy understanding and long-term memory retention of information that can be applied to any discipline.

Validated by various assessments, LEP teaching and learning methods have achieved immense success relative to significant increases in student engagement, course and learning outcomes, and in-class retention. But one of its greatest triumphs was recorded in long-term memory retention of material learned. Students assessed between 2012 to 2017 reported significant increases in long-term memory retention of material learned and were able to easily recall many facts and concepts learned long after taking the course. Additionally, whether in traditional or online settings, assessments concluded that utilizing LEP learning in the classroom has significantly enhanced the learning environment for both the educator and students.

The objective of this book is to provide a successful adaptable teaching tool for educators to use to engage students in opening their minds to an innovative teaching and learning method, which utilizes LEP's inquisitive reflection as an intentional instructor design to significantly enhance the learning environment and long-term memory retention of material learned. Further, the intention is to share with educators, for both food for thought and practical applications, the use of LEP teaching methods in the college classroom, either face to face or via technology, where students feel a part of the learning process, and mind maps unfold not only for the learner but also for the educator. It is often said that life is a journey. Why not then delve into that journey in a personal way in the classroom, whether in a traditional setting or online so that lived experiences are highlighted rather than ignored, creating a space within a learning environment where personal knowledge becomes not only relevant but also a useful instrument to assist in the understanding and retention of new learning. The LEP memory techniques included in this book that students will master will boost their overall learning and course outcomes, increase their engagement and participation, and significantly increase their comprehension and long-term memory skills.

LEP DEFINED

What can an experience be if it is not lived? Does just breathing constitute a lived experience if there isn't any meaning? Schutz (1967, pp. 69–71) contends that "meaning does not lie in the experience. Rather those experiences are meaningful which are grasped reflectively." He adds that "it is then, incorrect to say that 'my lived experiences' are meaningful merely in virtue of them being exercised or lived through. . . as it is the reflective glance that singles out an elapsed lived experience and constitutes it as meaningful." This means that the meaning of the "experience is essentially something constructed; it lies in what is made of—what is lived through" (Schutz, 1967), but it is how it is perceived that makes it meaningful, significant, and memorable, and determines the strength of the memory itself and the memory recall.

A person's memory records a lifetime of lived experiences and thoughts. It is a massive data bank with an organizational structure so that information can be stored and retrieved. The brain uses memory categories to file memories where they belong. Each lived experience is filed away in its separate category with other "like" memories and expands existing memories in that category as new information is absorbed.

Meaningful memories are categorized in long-term memory and are ready to be used when needed. In the 1920s Karl Lashley conducted a series of experiments in an attempt to locate the part of the brain where memories were stored. He concluded that memories are not stored in any single area of the brain but are instead distributed throughout it. These findings demonstrated that people's lived experiences are all recorded in the human brain and moved into long-term memory if they were meaningful in some manner but were filed in different categories and areas of the brain.

The lived experiences must be categorized in the mind and assigned meaning for learning and memory to occur. The effort placed in trying to remember certain information such as the use of memory hacks can significantly increase memory recall. However, in general, stronger personal connections are usually more meaningful, thus making stronger memories, which are easier to recall. How significant the experiences were to the person and the intensity with which they were processed will ultimately determine their memory strength and recollection. Negative events appear to be more memory potent as research indicates that people generally recall negative events more vividly and quickly than the positive ones (Ito, Larsen, Smith, & Cacioppo, 1998).

Lived experiences are comprised of constructs that are organized based on previous experiences. Schutz (1967) notes that the full meaning of experience is not just the immediacy of the lived moment but emerges from explicit retrospection where meaning is recovered and reenacted. This indicates that past lived experiences that have not been categorized cannot serve as a basis for the comprehension and understanding of new information because the lived experience must be processed and reflected upon even fleetingly for meaning to occur. Denzin (1992) contends that lived experience exists only as a representation and does not exist outside of memory. This is one of the reasons that memories can be fluid, modifiable, adjusted consciously or subconsciously, and used as a basis of understanding for future learning.

The relationship between memory and lived experience is an important aspect of LEP learning. Memory is an active process, and people choose what to remember and how they represent their lived experiences in their own memories. The ways individuals choose to remember is a cognitive, social, and emotional process in which the construction of memories (lived experiences) is an ongoing activity. It is important to note that the practice of memory construction is imaginative (Denzin, 2001) because people choose what to remember; thus, memory may not necessarily be credible or reflective of true events.

Memories are not just about recalling facts. Memories are also lived experiences that are filtered through our perceptions about those facts. Because the memory may not be a true representation of the "reality" of the lived experience, it is of no consequence to LEP learning if it is used to form new and correct understanding of the concept, and/or as memory hack to recall learned information later. Thus, because personal perception has now infiltrated the facts, the possibility of describing the lived experience with great precision and recalling every moment accurately is not usually possible or achieved by individuals when recalling information. However, when learning new information, it may not necessitate that the individual remembers actual facts of events or situations, because memory, accurate or not, can still be used as a point of reference to explain, expand, or offer new perceptions on incoming information.

A lived experience, true or not, can always be manipulated through imagination by the rememberer to explain and frame new information and assign it meaning to explain the concept, or use it as an LEP memory hack. When a memory is framed within the individual's existing knowledge, it now has meaning and can be integrated with new information, which will bring about new knowledge, form an expanded definition of the concept and its applications, and strengthen its capacity to be recalled when needed. Since memories, or imaginative situations, are just representations and not the factual events, they are often biased because the individual's subconscious mind uses a lens that sees life from a personal perception, personal viewpoint, which is usually more self-serving and curved to their advantage. Bartlett (1932, p. 205) contented that "elaboration and invention are common traits of ordinary remembering." Moreover, recollection is not merely reduplicative, but is socially influenced (Bartlett, 1932). That is, people engage in memory-making processes in which the individuals' lived experiences often reflect their social constructs that shape their memories (Barkley, 2008).

Feelings of the lived experience is connected to formalizing emotions to the memory and should always be considered with LEP teaching, learning, and memory techniques. Feelings of and about lived experiences are directly related to perception and are an undiscovered well of knowledge waiting to be used by the students for exploration, content connection, and/or as memory reinforcements of new knowledge. It is important that students not only focus on the event of the "lived experience" itself relative to the concepts under study, but that educators encourage them to give emotions and feelings associated with the lived experience proper consideration. This will allow students time to explore their memories to find the best lens in which to relate to and understand the new concept. It will also motivate students to dig deeper within their own memories and increase their critical thinking skills through the use of their imagination to explain the concept under study. Students are busy with their lives, and very few students view their lived experiences or feelings as important happenings and opportunities for learning or a resource available to them for long-term memory retention of material learned. Once they are exposed to the LEP techniques and see the immediate results, they will quickly utilize this very effective learning tool throughout their academic journey, strengthening their skills as they progress forward to completing their degrees.

LEP is engaging to students because rather than simply memorizing information, LEP teaches content and its applications through the students' own memories, their personal stories, their own lived experiences, and/or their imagination.

This allows students to build a strong path toward understanding the content better in a personal way and for the continuation of learning that builds upon existing memories (knowledge) to expand and create associations to form new knowledge. A personal memory hack that will allow them to easily retrieve the learned material when needed completes the LEP memory process.

Introducing students lived experiences as a learning tool into the curriculum will allow students to consistently accrue new information in a personal way, expand their existing knowledge base, and increase memory retention of information learned through their own LEP memory hacks. In today's world, students need to take a step back from technology as their first choice for information or rely on straight memorization to move forward in their academic life and plug in their efforts into their own inner world of lived experiences, the existing knowledge within them, their own well of memories that are just waiting to be retrieved and used. For each student there is no greater or richer wisdom than one's own lived experience, even if that experience must be molded through the imagination to understand the concept better and assist in the explanation of its application(s).

LEP AND INQUISITIVE REFLECTION

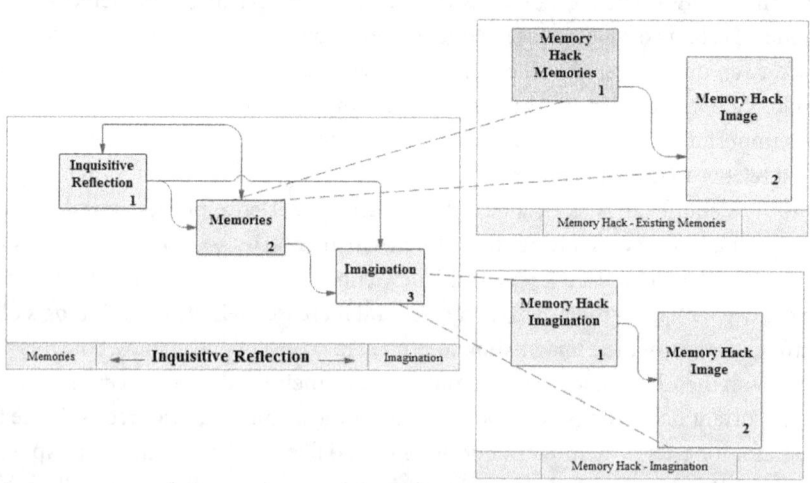

Students come complete with existing memories and imagination. Existing memories assist students to connect to new information using prior knowledge, and imagination uses academic interpretations to imagine scenarios in which the new information being learned can be understood or used. If prior knowledge relative to the topic studied is unavailable or cannot be accessed, or personal concept association by the student cannot be made, imagination is the instrument through which inquisitive reflection will be used. This means that the key tools in LEP learning and memory retention are both external and internal—external, such as knowledge imparted through textbooks, educators, and so on, and internal, using the brain to sift through existing information and employ inquisitive reflection to link information being learned in a personal way using prior memories or the imagination to connect to the concepts under study.

Reflecting in its simplistic form means looking back into the past. LEP's inquisitive reflection involves directed investigative inquiry of existing memories relative to the content under study, while looking back. LEP inquisitive reflection views memories as ready-to-use information housed in their separate categories. The space expands as new memories are formed and compared with archived items that are retrieved by students' minds from an inexhaustible storehouse. They include all memories, images, various information included by all the senses, innate learning attributes, lived experiences, messages, perceptions, interpretations, and so on, which are continuously received, often modified, and efficiently categorized. LEP's inquisitive reflection depends on these memories and uses them as influential and effective tools in the learning and long-term memory process.

"The power of memory is exceedingly great," wrote St. Augustine in *Confessions*. The philosopher describes memory as a place where people store their images, their entire life of experiences, and thought. He marveled at the vastness of this interior world. It is this world of memories that LEP taps into as its resource for personal learning.

"And so I come to the fields and vast palaces of memory, where are stored the innumerable images of material things brought to it by the senses. Further there is stored in the memory the thoughts we think, by adding or taking from or otherwise modifying the things that sense has made contact with and all other things that have been entrusted to and laid up in memory. . . . When I turn to memory I ask it to bring forth what I want: and some things are produced immediately, some take longer as if they had to be brought out from some more secret place of storage; some pour out in a heap, and while we are actually wanting and looking for something quite different, they hurls themselves upon us in masses as though to say: 'May it not be we that you want? I brush them from the face of my memory with the hand of my heart, until at last the thing I want is brought to light as from some hidden place. Some things are produced as required, easily and in right order and things that come first give place to those that follow and giving place are stored up again to be produced when I want them. . .' Memory is the locus of the self, the force that links present with past and gives identity." (St. Augustine, *Confessions*)

Memories can be intricate, deeply personal, or light hearted; irrespective, it is in the significance of the identity that memories give to all lived experiences as they are perceived by human beings that give it meaning. It is the identification of existing memories through that meaning that allows for growth and expansion of old information to include the new as it is processed through inquisitive reflection. The identification of the old information connects to new information and expands existing knowledge and understanding of the concept in a personal way, which makes it much easier to assign a memory hack to retrieve it later, as personal information often takes stronger and quicker root than academic knowledge.

LEP's inquisitive reflection is the continued and deep search to make a connection to concepts under study to find that memory that best suits the topic at hand, which can offer a foundation or expand the students' knowledge on the topic. It can weave new understanding of things experienced, change perceptions, and recreate the memory to achieve new learning because it is through the process of reflection that memories are brought forth and are available to be used. Margaret J. Wheatley concluded that "without reflection, we go blindly on our way, creating more unintended consequences, and failing to achieve anything useful."

All human beings need memories to learn from, and only through expanding our memories, we expand our knowledge. When that existing knowledge is unavailable or unattainable, unleashing the imagination to connect personal experiences to the content is a viable solution for students, which also greatly expands the concept's understanding and enriches the concept's application. Using the imagination to explain concepts vastly increases personal comprehension of the concept and assists memory retention of material learned.

Many educators and scholars agree that reflection whether through existing memories or through the imagination, which can be just as real to students, is an essential part of learning and an important vehicle to acquire knowledge. Since memories exist only in the past, LEP educators must promote reflective classrooms to ensure that their students are fully engaged in the process of making meaning through inquisitive reflection in which to understand and remember new information for the long term. Reflective classrooms encourage both reflections of the past to examine information and the use of imagination to explain the concepts' application(s). When memories are not available, students must be persuaded to use their imagination and creative visualization to link to the concepts to expand concepts applications. Whichever method is chosen students must be encouraged to get into the regular habit of using inquisitive reflection through either existing memories or their imagination to connect and construct meaning of new information and enhance their understanding of concepts being learned and to increase their long-term memory skills.

Teaching students how to inquisitively reflect is of utmost importance. Reflection is a means to discover and transform peoples' understanding (Mezirow, 1990). It is an exploration and explanation of data in a human's mind that is deliberate and structured in thinking. But reflections are not merely memories of how good or bad an experience was; instead, in reflection students must consider how the experience ties into the concepts being learned, and how this information can be remembered long term. Costa and Kallick (2008) contended that educators must assist students to construct meanings from the concepts learned and illustrate their various applications to other contexts or settings. In this way students will have access to examples that they could apply to their own lives, which would expand their understanding of the concept and offer various structural applications for them to review.

Inquisitive reflection allows for a meaning-making forum where critical thinking and applications take on a personal nature and are used to understand new information and as a resource to remember it long term. Students should be introduced to inquisitive reflection in the course as soon as realistically possible to allow them the full opportunity to master it by the time the course is over. When educators arm their students with the art of LEP's inquisitive reflection, they have armed them with a new tool of learning and long-term memory retention skills that can be used far outside of academics.

TEXTUAL AND STRUCTURAL FRAMING

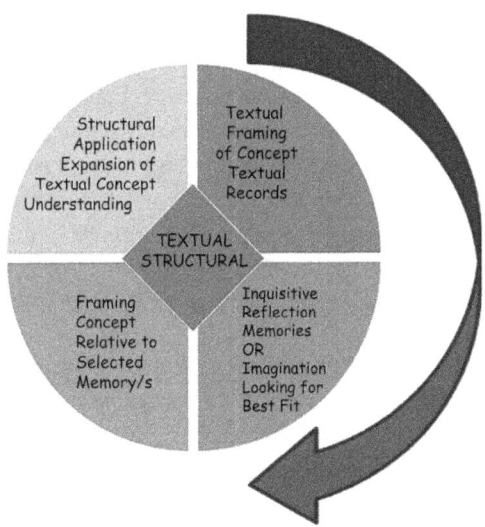

The combination of textual and structural framing vastly improves student understanding of concepts and memory retention of information learned. LEP's learning embraces these two processes because they build on each other to produce an expanded view of the concept's definition (textual) and applications (structural). In textual and structural framing, the goal is to identify the meaning of the concept as learned through textual information and include the structural essence of that concept through relational meaning to form a complete understanding and applications of the learned concept in a uniquely personal way, so that it is remembered and easily retrieved through LEP memory hacks. The structural essence that accompanies textual information underlies the completeness of the full understanding of the concept(s) under study.

Textual Framing

Textual framing is objective data that focuses on factual descriptions of the definition of the concept. In textual applications, students learn from any text, auditory, visual, and other formats as new information usually comes in through one of the senses and generates information about the topic under study. Textual framing such as traditional note taking is the most common, although not always the most effective, way to record information by students of all ages and demographic groups. Although written text is useful, it is usually not known for long-term retentiveness. The problem with focusing only on textual aspects, such as just noting the identification of concepts or memorizing textual information, is that students admit to forgetting everything they read unless it somehow made an impact on them, or they connected to it on some level.

Textual framing in the traditional sense is objective, intellectual reasoning of the information given. LEP textual framing shares this view but differs in that it offers an additional dimension of organizing information through a visual textual structure. Textual framing illustrates general ideas and identifies the definition of the analysis of the textual evidence as learned in more global term using resources such as notes from instructors' presentations, text book, handouts, and so on. It is a clear definition or description of the logical interpretation of the concept that is being digested in a textual form. At its basic function, textual framing when learning new information involves the student to decode information about the concept on a basic level and at least form a general opinion of the concept based on the information that has been presented.

LEP textual framing even though housed in the same objective of recording information for future use is a more creative process because it doesn't follow the linear way of taking notes by hand and recording as much of the information as possible or typing while information is flowing, such as during lecture, but instead adds a structural dimension for a deeper and more personal interpretation of the applications of the concept(s). LEP learning encourages students to apply creative and effective visual strategies which are included in this book, to supplement and reinforce the recorded information they need to know, understand, and remember. Students can easily record textual information in flow-based charts using key parts of paragraphs, creating images, sketches, graphs, diagrams, and so on in simple visuals to increase the comprehension and organizational structure of the content to emphasize the important details and not place much importance on the irrelevant. Textual information can also be bulleted or organized spatially with arrows connecting all relevant facts that describe the content being learned, or in any other visual manner the students prefer.

The LEP textual process embraces visual note taking and should be used in combination with structural framing to build on the information to further expand the understanding of the concept and its applications. The information can be easily connected by arrows to create structural interpretation that will vastly expand on textual knowledge. By connecting ideas that relate to each other, the end result is an organized mapping of the content under study and an easy way to understand and remember the new information.

Structural Framing

Building on textual knowledge, structural framing through inquisitive reflection adds to the understanding of the concept by offering support information that underlies and expands the concepts' meaning in a very personal manner leading to clearer concept applications. In this way, the students not only have the definition of the concept but are able to apply it in their life, which contributes to long-term memory retention of new information. The text is objective unbiased information; the structure is subjective, much more personal as it is a personal perspective the student gives the text to structurally represent its overall meaning and essence. It is a personal interpretation of what the concept means to them, with each interpretation having equal value, until the students place a different value, significance, or importance to it, or connect to new information in a new or expanded way.

LEP structural framing seeks to identify how new information fits into the world at large and to the students personally. It relies and uses all the senses of sensory memory, personality, and intelligence, and takes into consideration the overall makeup of the person and how they learn and remember information. Structural framing is intrinsic as it observes, seeks, explores emotions and feelings, and looks for essences of a thing, a relationship other than just basic interpretations of words or images, which is the job of textual framing. It is an internal mechanism that assists the students to perceive the information on a personal level as they extract relevant information from a stimulus, such as print in the textbook, and search their memories to detect a similar structure in which to connect to the concept under study.

In other words, the student not only adds structure to sensory stimulation (the written word) but detects the structure that already exists within their memory systems and expands the framework by integrating it with existing information to form a new concept structure (new understanding). By detecting information already existing in the students' memory, the students can see how the text being learned structures the information and how that information can be personally applied in their world. In doing this the students focus on the concept and its applicability to themselves, which peaks their interest, engages them in the material they are learning, expands textual knowledge, strengthens their memory retention, and assists them in a much quicker information retrieval of information when needed. The higher the level of activity on the students' part that expands the structural domains, the greater the understanding of the concept and memory recall, which stimulates automatic connection of the information, which can provide multiple memory retrieval paths for accessing the knowledge of the concept when needed.

Structural framing through inquisitive reflection captures the experience of learning and allows students to engage with their data and conclude how it applies to them, rather than just try to understand it passively. It offers the opportunity for students to experience new knowledge and see the concept in a variety of ways, through various sets of different experiences, and memories. It allows students to experience first-hand how the new knowledge can help them and offers them a moment to think how they feel about the relationship between themselves and the concept, and how they can best remember this information so that it may benefit them.

Combined textual and structural interpretations relative to the understanding of the concept and its applications is a highly effective learning process that educators should encourage in their classroom whether in a traditional manner or online to increase learning and memory retention of information learned. Practice in working with this process is integral to swift and significant success, and educators should incorporate short lesson plans, activities, or exercises within the classroom and online settings in which students have the opportunity to practice moving material from "content absorption" to "content connection" using LEP inquisitive reflection as a built-in process of learning in the course. Ask students often, even after you think they are comfortable with the process, to frame the concept you just presented using a personal narrative and what memories were triggered when they thought about the concept? Once practiced a few times, students will quickly get into the habit of searching their memories to connect to existing information and formulate a new personal understanding of the concept. As students begin to form an understanding of the concept through textual interpretation and expand their knowledge base, they may need assistance in drawing meaning from the concept learned; thus, the educator should step in and demonstrate ways in which the new information can be applied or operates in students' life or society at large.

Other times, when a memory may not be readily available for students to connect to, the educators should direct students to use their imagination and creative visualization as tools to apply to the concept as a starting point of personal understanding. Students should be patient and encouraged to play with their existing memories until the best memory fit that explains the concept is found, or use their imagination to frame their understanding of the concept. Playing with various scenarios by using inquisitive reflection allows students to be creative and enjoy the inquisitive reflection process while structuring the concepts to fit various existing memories that is the best fit for their recorded textual interpretations and retrieve it when needed.

Structural representations that best fit the concept can contain all sensory aspects, including feelings. Feelings as structural representations can be utilized to connect to the concept under study to answer the questions of when and how, as often insight gained through the exploration of feelings relative to the concept will greatly increase the student's range and depth of creative structural thinking and will assist in vast exploration of the existing information to a point of being able to select the best memory to use as a trigger to create a long-term memory hack that will help with the retrieval of information when it is needed. Using LEP's inquisitive reflection to create a better interpretation and frame a better understanding of the concepts students are learning will vastly assist them in the memory-encoding process and the ability to retain that information long term and retrieve it when needed.

LEP MEMORY HACK TOOL

The LEP Memory Hack Tool is a phenomenal instrument that has achieved success beyond all expectations in long-term memory retention and easy retrieval of information learned. The tool, in conjunction with the brain works to recognize familiar information and creates connections between new information and existing memories to form new knowledge that is easier to remember and retrieve when needed. Created to be used independently, in combination with each band, or as a complete step-by-step process to assist in the creation of memory triggers and hacks to remember and retrieve information, it has proven to be a powerful tool to improve and sharpen memory because of the personal connection to content being learned.

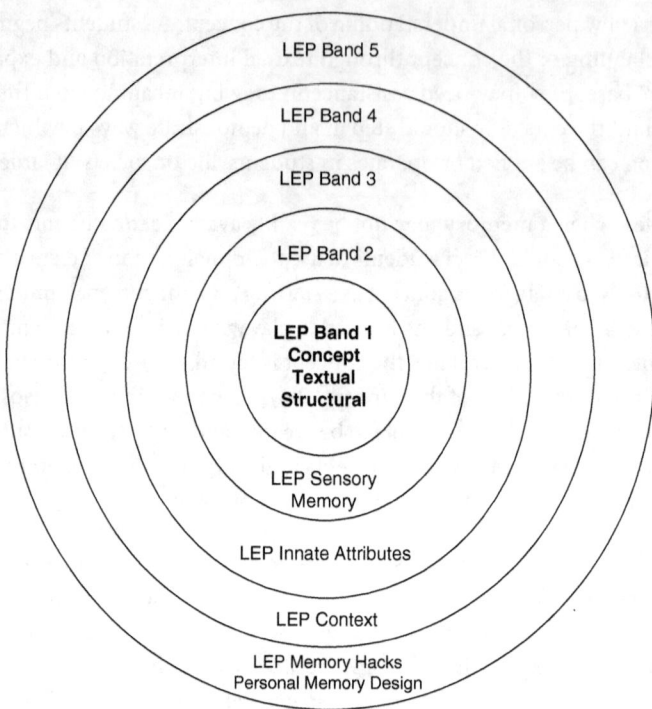

The LEP Memory Hack Tool consists of five bands that can be used to learn, remember, and retrieve the learned information. The first band includes the initial acquisition of knowledge and is the space where new information is received and processed through textual and structural framing for an expanded understanding, which includes not only textual description of content but personal application(s), and long-term retention of the new information. It is the first stage in which new information is received and processed through the combined textual (text) and structural (application) framing approaches and the organization of new information so that it is easily understood from external and internal approaches. The second band includes the first of the three LEP memory trigger categories, Sensory Memory. LEP Sensory Memory Triggers include the five senses of sight, hearing, taste, smell, and touch. Sensory memory triggers are a key category in learning and retaining new information because human experiences are processed through sensory systems. The third band holds the second LEP memory trigger category, LEP Innate Attributes. LEP Innate Attribute triggers include Linguistic/Word Attribute, Logical Attribute, Musical Attribute, Interpersonal Attribute, Intrapersonal Attribute, Naturalistic Attribute, Existential Attribute, and the Spiritual Attribute (holistic) trigger. Students learn in a way that is unique to them through their own innate personal attributes. Attributes, in a sense, are human beings natural learning predispositions, meaning that students learn in various ways that they are naturally predisposed to and tend to perceive information through that lens.

The fourth band hold the third and last LEP memory trigger category LEP Personal Life Contexts. The LEP Personal Life Contexts include the Physical Context Triggers, Emotional Context Triggers, Mental Context Triggers, Environmental Context Triggers, Spiritual/Religious/Universal Context Triggers, and the Moral Context (conscience) Triggers. LEP Personal Life Contexts categorize memory triggers through various contextual elements which focus not only on the definitions but on the structure of concepts from a personal lived experience knowledge and perspective which greatly aids concept application processes. In addition, to forming memory hacks to retrieve information, the fifth band, LEP Personal Memory Design Patterns completes the process and includes the patterns of organizing information visually through the following organizational patterns; chronological, sequence, cause and effect, problem and solution, and compare and contrast to visually organize information for easy comprehension. The LEP Memory Hack Tool will be explained in detail in later chapters.

CHAPTER TWO

SETTING THE LEP LEARNING TONE

> SETTING THE LEP TONE IN THE CLASSROOM AND ONLINE
> MIND-SHIFT FROM "CONTENT ABSORPTION" TO "CONTENT CONNECTION"
> LEP MIND MAPPING

SETTING THE LEP TONE IN THE CLASSROOM AND ONLINE

Setting the LEP tone in the classroom and online as with any course requires adequate course preparation. That in itself is not new, as every successful course requires some type of planning. What makes the setting for LEP teaching and learning unique is that it also requires a "buy-in" to the LEP learning and memory process. The "buy-in" process includes both the educator and students. Within the LEP process, educators must be prepared to teach and students must be prepared to learn, from this backward-to-forward approach, share personal information relative to the concepts learned, and feel safe in doing so, regardless if the classroom is a physical setting or online.

If educators are asking students to "buy in" and share personal information, they must be willing to share themselves. The educator is the strongest presence and influence in the course, and regardless of the setting must show the "buy-in" by responding in a personal way to the material imparted. This should include personal demonstrations to explain not only the concepts but also its applications that show students the relevancy of what they are learning. Most educators are already presenting new information in this way, without realizing that they are already teaching with the LEP process; thus, this should not be a far reach for most educators.

The educator is the project coordinator and facilitator of the learning process and, as such, sets the tone of the classroom. Thus, educators must be adequately prepared to create and manage the learning climate for their students, whether that is in the traditional classroom or in a virtual environment throughout the length of the course. LEP educators should always be thinking of the next lesson and how to best reach their students to connect them to the information they are learning on a personal level and empower them with the knowledge they need to be successful in academia and beyond. They know that planning and preparing for each class goes well beyond the creation of lesson plans and sets the tone to include ways to engage students to their top learning potential by using their existing memories as resources for new knowledge.

Setting the tone also includes being organized and having the appropriate supplemental resources available during lessons. Course preparation, in most traditional and online courses, includes updating resources such as unit outlines, PowerPoints, and refreshed assignments and adding new video collections, revised tests, updated handouts, worksheets, and so on. This is true in any classroom, including one taught with LEP teaching methods because students need organization and outside resources like handouts to clarify and work with the information under study.

Because the LEP learning and memory process of using the students' own memories to learn new information is one students are not usually familiar with, they will need strong and consistent guidance. Assessments taken from 2012 to 2017 include the findings that students grasp the LEP learning and memory process quickly, with most mastering it within a few short weeks. The worksheets included in this book are a good place to start to introduce students to the LEP learning and memory retention process of material learned. The worksheets are deliberately left basic, just offering the basic idea so that that the LEP educators may get the benefits of creating their own according to the needs of their course(s). Each LEP educator should modify, adjust, or create new LEP worksheets, handouts, and so on to fit his or her idea of how to best draw personal information from students to connect to the content they are teaching.

LEP educators must emphasize and encourage the use of LEP from the onset of the course and continue the LEP tone in the classroom for the duration of the course. Even greater efforts should take place online, as LEP's presence must be felt in a personal way between the educator and learners, and between learners and learners, so that they may share without inhibitions, learn the material, and learn from each other. This must start with the educator and their ability to share information using their personal examples when demonstrating concepts and their applications.

This combined network of interaction and conversations that can be steered through blogs and discussion boards where everyone shares their personal experience relative to the information they are learnings for greater expansion of the application of the concepts under study must be fostered for the length of the course for students to stay engaged and meet learning outcomes. The more students use LEP, the quicker they will see results and be more comfortable with the LEP learning and memory retention process. This is true for both traditional classroom and online courses even though online students may need more guidance with additional uploaded resources, materials, and more personal interactive communication.

The process of LEP learning approach should be included in the syllabus. Students should be informed of the requirements, expectations and benefits of LEP learning in writing so that they are prepared in advance that personal information relative to the concepts they are learning will be shared. Studies show that students perceive the tone of the class (Harnish & Bridges, 2011) and often the personality of the instructor (McKeachie, 1986) by the syllabus and, therefore, can create a first impression about the educators' attitudes toward students and learning (DiClementi & Handelsman, 2005). Thus, it is imperative that educators outline the LEP learning and memory retention process in the syllabus and include motivational language encouraging students to fully participate citing the many benefits gained through learning and retaining information learned through LEP.

Since LEP is a personal approach to learning, students should be made aware of the depth they will be asked to delve for information within themselves while learning new information. Thus, LEP's presence in the syllabus must be felt. LEP online courses must also include a detailed explanation of LEP learning and memory retention process clearly informing students as to what to expect and how LEP works. Examples and samples of the LEP learning and memory process as it pertains to specific courses should be available and include the expectations of utilizing their existing memories and lived experiences to learn and remember new information.

Whether in a traditional or an online setting, preparing for an LEP course is involved because of the added focus on personal connections between the subject matter and the students. But the benefits of significantly higher learning and course outcomes, in-class retention, and increased student engagement and long-term memory of information learned by the students far outweigh the educators' time involved. And even though, at first, the LEP learning and memory retention process may take a little practice, with the educators' guidance, and in a relatively short time, the students will master the process easily.

As essential as planning is of equal importance is the right mix of intellectual resources provided in the course and the educators' encouragement for students to persevere and continue to use the LEP memory process in their learning throughout the duration of the course. Encouraging students and using the educators' own personal examples will make learning much more meaningful because the students will see a relationship between content taught and themselves, and the educator as a caring asset in their learning process. In this way the educator paves the way for learning based on cooperation and collaboration, where information is shared in a supportive environment rather than hierarchy with the educators on the top and the students below them.

The goal of LEP teaching and learning is to maximize the interaction between educators and learners, and learners and learners, and information and learners. This collaborative tone creates a psychological atmosphere that promotes learner growth, which enjoys and sees the value of learning. Thus, all educators can successfully embrace LEP teaching, which will result in significant increases in students' engagement and learning and memory retention.

LEP learning can be looked upon as a pedagogical model that sets the tone for students to learn through both external (intellectual) and internal (emotional) needs. This means that students are learning at an intellectual level, are remembering the information, and are emotionally satisfied because they see results and the value of learning in LEP's personal way. At an external level the classroom tone and environment become important aspects in the learning environment, and educators must create an active, supportive, and trusting learning setting that allows for self-discovery and growth, where personal experiences shared as related to concepts being learned assist in the students' understanding and often their classmates' learning process. At an internal level the satisfaction of progress and increases in test scores motivate students to shift themselves to think in reflective ways. Additionally, from a students' perspective, understanding not only the concepts but also their applications in a personal way vastly increases self-esteem and value for the dollar spent on education.

LEP teaches from a backward to a forward lens and from the perception of valuing and embracing students' lived experiences and tying these valuable memories, which they store in their mind warehouses to the course content for increased understanding and long-term memory retention. Traditionally, learning is slated more to the present and the future as opposed to the past. Students learning in this orientation do not look back; rather they look forward to finding information. In these scenarios, educators and students abandon past lived experiences and move forward without reflecting on the seemingly independent and unrelated experiences of the past that are such valuable opportunities for current and future learning. Moreover, LEP's backward-to-forward approach maximizes the interaction between the learners and the information they are learning, educators and learners, and learners and learners. Experiences that relate to the concept are shared either in the classroom or through discussion boards online, immensely contributing to the textual and structural interpretation of the concepts under study and often adding to the learning community feel that students crave.

For educators especially, sharing your story and being mindful that first impression counts are important factors in how well the course will progress throughout the semester. Long-term student retention starts with the first day of class because first impressions have a major impact on college students' attitudes, and can greatly impact the tone, course outcomes, and students' interest level. Setting the tone for the class should begin with a feel of a dynamic environment on the onset in which students are engaged and look forward to because this will result in significant increases in student retention, higher learning, and course outcomes. Thus, it is very important for educators to introduce the process of LEP learning and memory retention as part of the learning setting in the course as soon as possible and begin sharing themselves. Additionally, students should always be provided with a guide sheet included in this book, or one that educators create to help them get started and stay on track using the LEP process as soon as possible.

By introducing LEP early, the educator will frame the class experience at the start and teach students to begin to mind-shift from "content absorption to content connection" without delay. A "different" beginning, a fresh personal approach that lasts throughout the duration of the semester could make all the difference in students' engagement levels and the effort spent on the material being learned. Some educators already incorporate short interpersonal exchanges when teaching whether through offering personal perspective to tie into the concept they are explaining, or to clarify a point, but LEP teaching methods insist that educators invest greater energy, dig deeper, and place a true emphasis on the importance of the lived experience as a resource in understanding and remembering the content under study.

LEP learning empowers students to understand information using their own personal lens of understanding. When students begin to understand what they are learning through a personal lens and can apply it to themselves or the world at large, they have mastered the definitions and applications of the concepts. This will assist in the "buy-in" that this course and what they are learning is valuable to them, which, in turn, will increase students' engagement and retention rates, and significantly boost test scores and learning outcomes and long-term memory retention.

In short, in order to set the tone for sharing, educators must set the precedent and begin to share themselves.

> **Your Story**: Start by telling your story. Stories have a profound effect on students' understanding of information learned and memory retention, especially stories that offer humor and relatable situations. So why not engage students on a personal level and allow them to get to know you. This personal bond will assist in class retention later. So, share and let the LEP educator and student relationship flourish and bloom, and watch as the classroom environment begins to transform from one of "when is this class over" to "I can't believe this class is already over."

The information shared does not have to be very personal, but personally applicable to the concepts learned. Basic everyday facts are just as interesting and engaging. It is important that students relate to their LEP educators as more than just authority figures or subject matter experts, but as people who have experiences that they remember and learn from, just like themselves.

It may seem awkward at first to share personal details about who you are and your own "lived experiences," but relating them to the concepts under study opens up a brand new opportunity for students to learn about the concept from your experience and see it in new light. If you seek later to ask your students to tap into their lived experiences, sharing yours, at the beginning of the course, and then as appropriate, throughout the course, can clearly demonstrate to your students that you do value these experiences, that they are a part of the learning journey, and that they can use these skills to learn and remember information not only in this course but beyond. The classroom can become welcoming and warm in this manner, highlighting that teaching and learning is a reciprocal fascinating process and that the course can be a new exciting learning adventure not only for meeting course and learning outcomes and attaining long-term memory skills, but also for enjoyment in seeing the value of what they are learning, self-discovery, and students' personal growth.

> **Their Stories:** Students should be consistently sharing their stories as they relate to the concepts learned whether that is during class time, in assignment, or online. To initiate the sharing of the students' stories in class, where time may be a factor, it is best to keep things short and structured. At first to demonstrate LEP the educator may initiate discovery by asking the students to introduce themselves and pick one thing about their life relative to why they are taking the course to share in class. The educator may also choose any topic related to the course and ask students to reflect on what they know about it to illicit a discussion.

With every experience shared, the understanding of the topic and its applications will most likely be expanded. Another approach is for the educator to ask students to turn to another student in class and share this information for a smaller setting approach through a short discussion format. This is a fun exercise that can create bonds of friendships at the beginning of the course and socialization that may assist with finding a study partner and a friendlier classroom environment for the student—which may assist in student retention and engagement.

Although these activities are designed to get to know students personally and rely on lived experiences, it should be reiterated to students that the information sought to explain concepts should not be "deeply personal" and, as such, should not include any questions or responses that would make anyone uncomfortable. The questions should come from the content connection perspective relative to their life. A simple approach to keep things very general and quick, at the beginning of the course, is to ask students to take a moment and write down answers to the question of: "How do I best learn?" This will help them become aware of the qualities they already have to approach LEP learning and so that they can be introduced to sharing information about themselves. The educator can highlight the various choices by students and talk about how learning from lived experiences will take place in the classroom and how their learning abilities can assist them to use the LEP learning and memory processes to their highest potential.

Consider your student audience in every case and adjust accordingly, as every class is different in a myriad of ways. The above approach can also work with online courses but must be modified, since the students are not physically present. Thus, in an online setting the same discussion can be originated but through different means such as discussion boards or blogs. The discussion should always be inviting and relevant to the information the students are learning and should actively seek involvement from all students. (Of course, the easiest way to ensure cooperation and engagement is to assign a weighed grade to the assignment.)

Setting an acceptance of a sharing LEP tone in the classroom in traditional settings and online is the fresh approach that is not only needed, but also necessary. It must be understood that it will require a learning curve for both educators and students as there are some complexities involved as in any teaching and learning method. But if LEP educators are prepared and plan ahead, the benefits to students' and educators' own growth, combined with vastly increased learning and course outcomes, and long-term memory retention of information learned, quickly outweigh any challenges.

Figure 2.1 Content Absorption to Content Connection Process

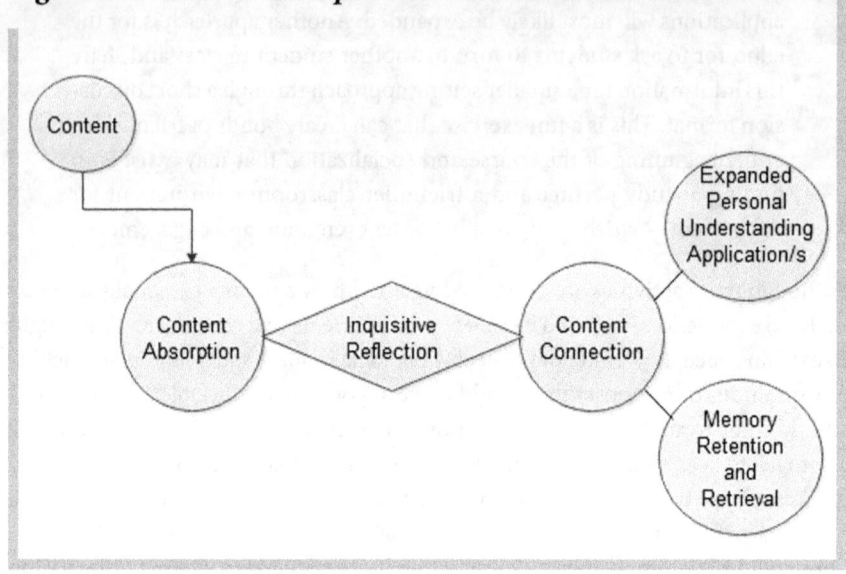

MIND SHIFT FROM CONTENT ABSORPTION TO CONTENT CONNECTION

Before beginning any course or preparation, a mind shift from "content absorption to content connection" (see figure 2.1) must occur within the educator. The mind shift is imperative so that he or she may comfortably work with the LEP learning and memory process and guide his or her students to mind shift themselves to achieve optimal results in learning and memory retention of learned information. Moreover, it is recommended that LEP educators subscribe to the mind-mapping platform of visual introduction or presentation of information whenever possible and use it diligently throughout the course as its visual features vastly assist students to organize information for comprehension and memory retention purposes.

LEP educators should continuously strive for a reflective tone both in the classroom and in the virtual settings as reflective LEP teaching and learning does not just happen automatically. This is why it is so important for the educator to put conscious effort to change the mind shift from "content absorption" to "content connection" within their own mind on the onset of the preparation of and planning for course. The educator who embraces the concept of LEP teaching methods must shift in thinking and needs to move from the mindset of "I have this information to impart upon to these students for them to absorb" to "the students bring to class a wealth of life experiences upon which I can draw upon to connect them to new learning, creating the opportunity for a transformative process of meaning for each of them as they go through the course, stay engaged, learn, remember and enjoy the experience enough to move forward in their academic career." This is a monumental mind shift, but educators have within themselves the ability to mind shift, to move from traditionally held views of learning to a more dynamic outlook on what the college classroom using LEP in both the traditional and online formats can offer, and the best way to utilize this living resource.

LEP educators must consistently reinforce the mind shift from "content absorption" to "content connection" in their students until learning with the LEP process becomes a natural and innate learning skill within them. Through regular practice and use, educators can help their students create formative results, leading to increased critical and reflective thinking skills, and increased understanding and application of concepts through purposeful personal meaning which increases understanding and long-term memory retention of the studied concepts. The information is easier to learn and recall because it is reinforced through the meaning and interpretation of the concept learned in a very personal way. Whenever a person speaks, sees, reads, listens to, or observes anything, he or she experiences a lived experience. The mind absorbs this sensory data, stores it, and, if coded properly, has it available for retrieval for future use whenever it is summoned. Students must be reminded to continuously connect to this personal database of existing information that they all possess in their memory storage and retrieve information from the past that can help them in the present.

The mind learns, and the mind remembers. The mind is a miraculous warehouse, and the typical college classroom does not tap into the depths of dimensions that are possible through understanding and remembering information through personal meaning. Using LEP teaching and learning, educators are asking students to not only absorb the information presented but also connect to the information personally using their memories to expand the understanding and interpretation of the concepts they are learning. Students are asked to summon memories of lived experiences and lessons they have derived through their lived experiences, and to apply those elements to the concepts they are learning in their college classrooms to expand the definitions and applications of the concept(s), problem solve, compare and contrast, and so on.

This is a powerful use of the extraordinary minds of our students. They have these lived experiences, memories, within each of them, they just need to connect to them and use them for future learning. LEP harnesses that information for continued growth, which flows from the lived experience and connects to concepts within the college environment, and beyond. The idea is powerful when one really considers it, and the implications for personal learning and memory retention of material learned within the college classroom both in a physical setting and online are enormous.

Thus, it is vital that educators are able to shift to this recognition, to think about how what they are teaching, and how each student can learn to embrace this backward-to-forward lens and how best they can assist students to mind shift from content absorption to content connection as well. Students are always asked to learn new material and study new concepts. But they are not asked to go back into their own minds to lived experiences only they can know, to make this leap and use this living resource, their lived experience, as content expansion and a memory retention tool. The college classroom educator as a guide and facilitator, along with being the course discipline expert, should always reflectively think about how the minds of his or her students can be opened in this way.

As students are asked to delve into their existing memories to find the understanding of new information and new concepts, and activating and connecting content to memory, it is worth asking questions to ensure that the educator is at their strongest in this process, such as "How do I bring the lives and experiences of my students into the classroom, connect it to the content being learned, and keep them on point once they get there?" "How do I frame the concept for optimal understanding by the students?" and "What format should I use to deliver each lesson for optimal results—class discussion, written assignment, lecture, group work or a combination of these? What is the best way I can teach them to trigger their existing memories to the concepts that I am teaching? How can I show them through personal examples on how to create the best memory trigger to understand new information, and memory hacks for retrieval of that same information when needed? Questions such as these become imperative for the educator and relevant learning takes on a much more important meaning.

LEP educators must embrace the mind shift and be willing to change and learn. Be open to everything the LEP teaching and learning methods have to offer. The mind shift in thinking from content absorption to content connection necessitates pre-course thought and planning by the educator and additional effort to weave LEP in and out of the course to increase content understanding and long-term memory retention of information learned, but it is well worth the effort.

Content Absorption to Content Connection

Through content absorption to content connection, LEP takes learning and memory to a whole new level, where learning is an enjoyable activity for students and memory retention becomes personal. This occurs through not only absorbing the content, meaning being acquainted with new information through lecture, book, and so on, but also having the ability to connect to it from a personal level to gain a better understanding of its application and how that concept plays out in the students' life or the world at large. LEP inquisitive reflection significantly increases the understanding of new information through the process of "content absorption" to a "content connection" approach, where students learn new information in a unique way and have the ability to easily recall it later.

It is important to note that LEP inquisitive reflections are not lengthy life chronicles but are directed and structured to focus selectively and directly on the concepts at hand. The students inquisitively reflect zeroing in only on the concept under study, making appropriate constructs that accurately reflect the understanding of the concepts through a personal lens. LEP inquisitive reflection helps students see things in new ways and how the information they are learning about applies to them personally, which renders exercises in inquisitive reflection very useful tools and the activity itself something they are excited about doing.

At a closer look, content absorption includes textual interpretations of concept descriptions and the initial reaction of "what" and "why," and sometimes "who." Content connection involves structural interpretation and is directed more to the "when" and "how," but can also encompass "where," to give concepts additional structural meaning. The initial process begins with textual acquisition of new information and is followed by inquisitive reflections to structurally connect to the concept.

CONTENT ABSORPTION

- **Content absorption:** Textual acquisition. In the initial description state the information is introduced to the student and content absorption is initialized. Initial description focuses on textual acquisition of the basic knowledge of the concept, meaning that new information that is received through any sensory means is recorded. In this state the students take notes and can explain the concept in textual generic terms based on the information received from the educator, textbooks, and so on. At the end of this exercise, they should have the general understanding of the concept.

    (Students at the textual descriptive state have limited perceptions relative to new information presented. At this state, educators should explain the concepts thoroughly using visuals, lecture, priming, discussion, reading assignments, and so on to introduce and explain the concept to the students in varied ways to accommodate a greater range of student learning preferences. The concepts should be described using the academic interpretation and students should be offered at least one real-life applicable example they can record next to their notes as a clarification point).

- **Content absorption: What and why?** The educator should gauge students' reaction to new information at the initial description stage. At first glance how do the students relate to the information imparted? Does the information feel like it resonates? To gauge how the information is perceived, the educator should encourage students to share a quick snapshot of their thoughts as to how they are relating and absorbing this information and to record their thoughts in their notebooks, or electronic devices as a means to expand concept definitions. Recording and updating the information as new data is received is the beginning of absorbing the information, and expanding and building upon existing knowledge, which regularly results in clear and concise notes that can easily be used in preparation for tests or assignments later. Often students build upon their existing notes throughout the duration of the course and in the end have a complete study guide to use for assorted tests and finals.

To keep thoughts simple and organized in the initial textual description during content absorption, students should focus on two simple facts, "what" and "why." It is not restricted, however, and other questions such as "who" may also be asked, but at first glance "what and why" should be sufficient to begin the textual description/interpretation of the concept process. What is the concept they are learning, and why do they personally care? Placing the importance on the basics, of what is it they are studying, and why, increases their understanding and allows for the personal application of the concept in their life, setting the stage for the LEP structural interpretations that follows textual interpretations.

A visual example of the content absorption textual activity is presented in figure 2.2. Students describe their understanding of the concepts by answering the questions of what? and why? and record the answers in the call-outs.

Figure 2.2 Content Absorption

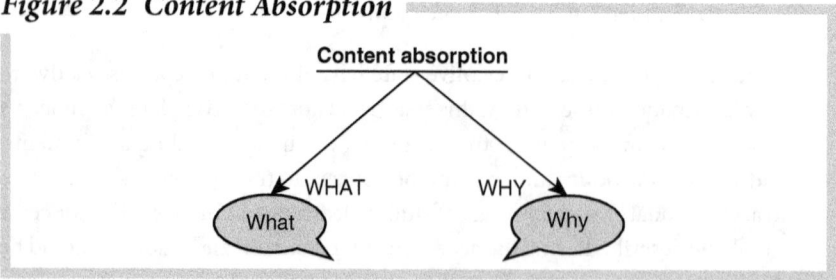

Textual interpretation (absorption) is followed by inquisitive reflection's structural interpretation of "when and how?" Inquisitive reflection interpretations move new information in the brain from content absorption to content connection as students personally identify with the information (textual) and can apply it (structural) in their life or the world at large. In the LEP learning and memory processing, initial textual descriptions are expanded to include structural interpretations to frame the concepts and provide either new or expanded understanding of concept.

Content Connection

Content connection involves searching existing memories to create structural constructs to better interpret concepts under study as outlined in the textual interpretations. Structural interpretation constructs allow for framing around the essence of the concepts, expands application understanding and is a creative way in which students can assimilate and apply new information in a uniquely personal way. LEP inquisitive reflection uses structural formats as a technique used to describe the field of meaning of something. This natural approach brings about personal applications of the concepts and its narrative and allows students to process information by having a personal point of reference in addition to academic concept descriptions or interpretations.

Content Connection—Structural Interpretations: When and How? Allows for Expansion of Textual Interpretations

Content connection involves structural information to expand on textual identifications and interpretations and often answers the questions of "when" and "how," and sometimes "where." As students search their memories to link the concepts for expanded understanding, they should be reminded that the relevancy of whether the information they are retrieving from their memories is true or not is of no consequence, only that it expands their knowledge base relative to the concept being learned in an authentic manner as it applies to the true definition of the concept. When and how offer a deeper structural characterization of the concepts under study and expand thoughts to allow for various applications to increase the understanding of the what and why of textual processing, which significantly increases overall understanding and vastly assists with concept application and memory retention of the new information learned.

Figure 2.3 presents an activity in which students can describe a structural essence of a concept in the call-outs by answering the questions of When? and How?

Figure 2.3 Content Connection

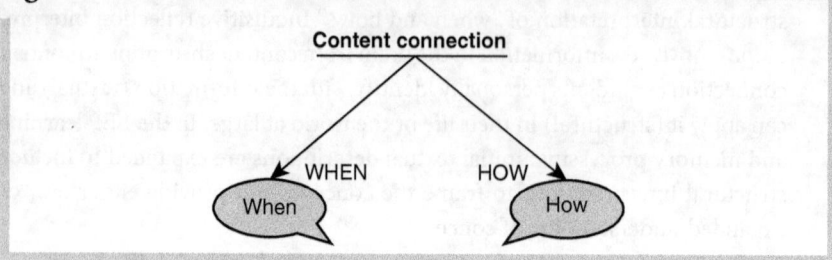

LEP MIND MAPPING

In LEP, mind mapping captures a natural way of thought progression and visually organizes incoming information. LEP teaching and learning both encourages and relies on the mind-mapping approach of visual learning to organize information for comprehension and memory retention. A mind map is a visual diagram that is utilized to organize information (Hopper, 2015) and is an integral tool within the LEP learning and memory retention process. Mind mapping is one of the best ways to capture ideas, thoughts, concepts, and relatable personal connections to the content under study because it quickly organizes information at a glance. Many students are visual and understand concepts with greater ease visually, rather than in an auditory lecture format. Mind mapping is an effective learning tool to help students brainstorm any subject and think creatively because it allows students to see the whole picture and how different thoughts and ideas stemming from the same concept are linked together. Visual information is also easier to remember when needed later.

LEP mind mapping connects content being learned to meaningful memories stored in the students' brain that can be used in current and future learning. Meaningful learning connects the content under study to personal information, which leads to long-term memory retention. Mezirow (1990) contends that meaningful learning is guided by experience and the interpretation of that experience, which is a process of revising the interpretation of an experience that leads to new ways of thinking, valuing, and acting. The expansion of knowledge leads to greater understanding, application, and memory retention of information learned.

LEP mind maps visually harness the full range of the concepts under study in a personal way using both textual and structural interpretations, thus giving students information through interpretations at a glance, which includes both the description and applications of the concept(s). There are numerous mind-mapping activities educators have to choose from when developing their courses. Educators may choose from any of the LEP mind-mapping content memory retention activities included in the book to incorporate in their lesson plan, modify the existing activities for their particular discipline, or create and customize their own (recommended). LEP educators should always encourage students to get into the mind-mapping practice and create their own mind maps as the content is being taught, or as they are listening to a lecture, as a note-taking technique.

Mind-mapping concepts through story creation is also another way to understand and remember information. Mind mapping the content through stories works particularly well with LEP when trying to understand and remember information because stories are an effective way to expand on existing memories and are usually a good vehicle to remember information. Students remember stories more readily than facts and are much more interested in what the professor is discussing if the information is related to personal experiences, or if the content they are learning holds personal meaning for them. Bough (2015) contends that stories are key in linking different events together that might have been lost in memory over time. LEP uses these links to expand on concept definition and offers a fresh new understanding of the concept and its applications in the students' life.

For centuries, stories have been and still are an effective teaching method because of their appeal to the larger population with various cognitive-processing levels and the ability to expand on the existing information to form new understanding. Stories are a means to present concepts and new information and help organize information being learned. Bough (2015) calls stories the foundation of knowledge, in which we build new memories to add to the existing knowledge. Thus, story mind maps can be continuously modified to incorporate new information to gain a clearer understanding of the whole concept. Bough (2015, p. 6) further contends that "our brains are wired for stories, and we do not easily remember what others have said unless it is in the form of story."

Because in LEP stories relative to concepts being learned are real lived experiences or are created through the imagination of the student they are much more personal than stories of strangers which increase the bond between the teacher and the students. Educators are encouraged to harness their own storytelling power to use in their courses to reach more students, which will increase learning outcomes and provide a richer learning experience and increased student engagement in the classroom and long-term memory retention of the material being learned. The more skillful the educator is at connecting information with personal relevance to the students, the more vivid the picture is painted in the students' mind, and the greater the understanding of the information. The more common the experiences and perceptions the educator uses in explaining the concept, the more "lights" the story turns on in the students' mind and the easier it will be for students to connect to if for personal relevancy. Thus, the more skillful the educator is throughout the duration of the course in relating their own lived experiences relative to the topics taught, and how each concept could be mind mapped for clarity and memory retention, the greater the chances that students will be able to use the LEP process easily themselves, and learn and remember the information long term.

Keeping it simple, at first, is always best. When constructing LEP mind maps, students should be directed to begin with a central concept and expand outward to more in-depth sub-topics and ideas that will surface. A good visual is to have students connect sub-topics and points of importance with arrows stemming from the central concept showing the relationship to the concept. In this way the understanding of the concept(s) increase but the application of how the concepts can be used in the real world also become evident.

Because mind maps promote the use of single key words, sketches, symbols, or shortened descriptions instead of whole sentences, students are able to review the concepts and applications at a glance and see the overall relevance to their lives as a whole. Students can detect hierarchies between individual pieces of information and attribute personal relevance and meaningful links to the concept. Additionally, the visual aspects of an LEP mind map along with their recorded personal lived experiences will reinforce the content in their long-term memory and is an ideal platform to create LEP memory hacks to retrieve the information later. When presenting material that will be transformed to mind maps, LEP educators always need to think one step beyond the content of the discipline and ask, "How can I link this concept to the lived experiences of my students so that they can easily mind map the new learning? How can I help them make that connection for themselves and enrich the work they do in my class through mind mapping the content to enhance learning?"

While course design is a professional exercise undertaken by the educator, infusing LEP is not always an easy route to visualize. However, in a short time, as LEP teaching and learning is included in classroom settings, and students regularly share their lived experiences relative to what they are learning, and are able to easily mind map the information, educators will see how readily students are able to make connections between themselves and their course work and create personal mind maps that will expand the concepts' definition and improve their learning outcomes and long-term memory retention. Mind maps, lived experiences, and memories can be quickly organized to shed light on concepts under study and offer a genuine connection to the subject matter and the opportunity to retain the information long term. Keeping it simple and clear is the optimal way to begin (see figure 2.4).

Figure 2.4 Simple Mind Map

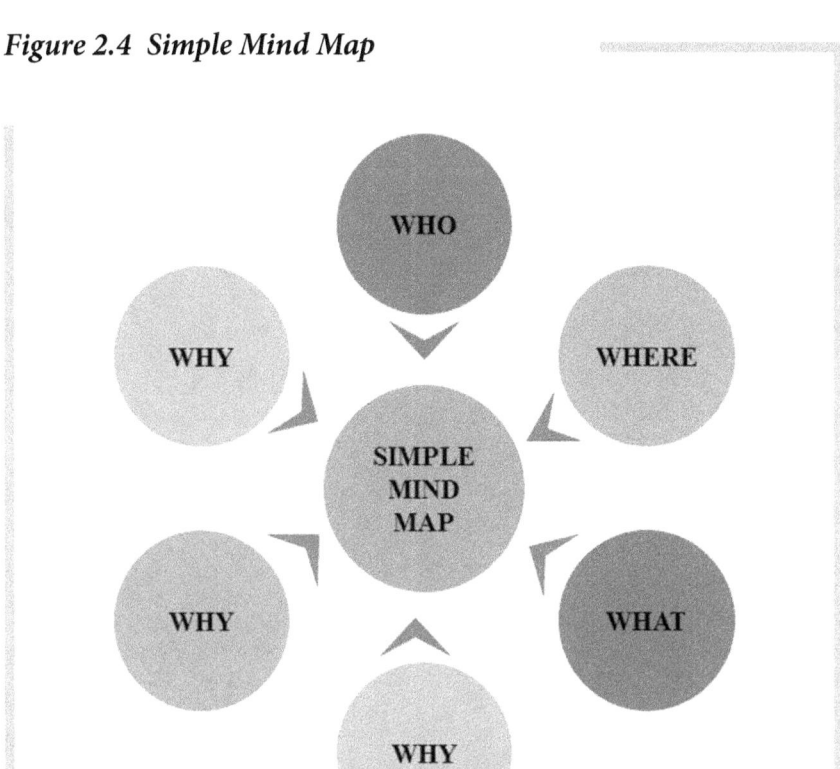

CHAPTER THREE

MEMORY SYSTEMS

INFUSING LEP IN THE COLLEGE CLASSROOM
THROUGH MEMORY SYSTEMS
LEP AND SENSORY MEMORY
LEP AND SHORT-TERM MEMORY
LEP AND LONG-TERM MEMORY
LEP AND EXPLICIT MEMORY
LEP AND IMPLICIT MEMORY
LEP PROCEDURAL MEMORY
PRIMING
FRAMING

LEP Memory Process Chart

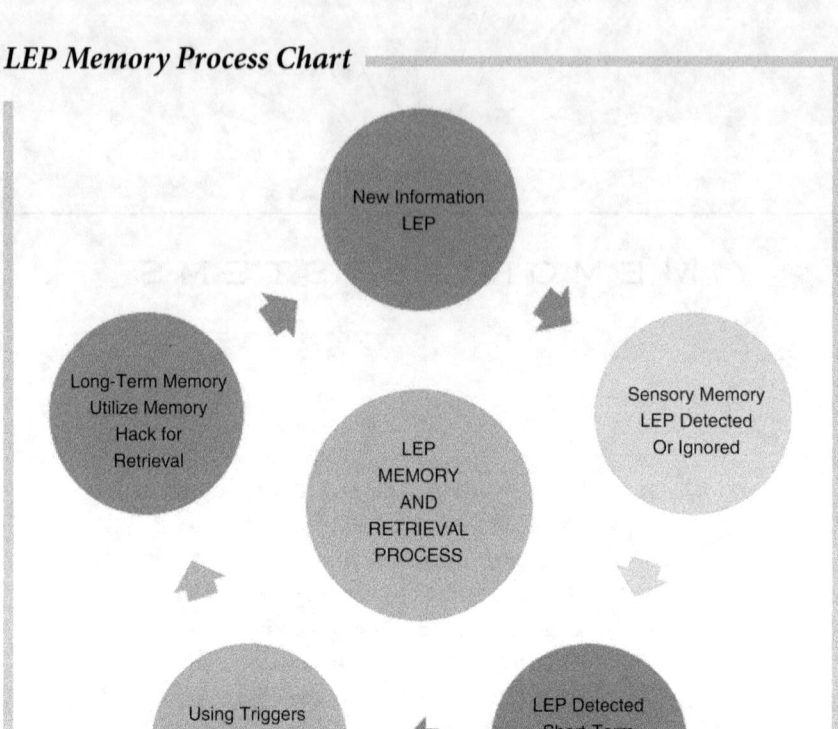

INFUSING LEP IN THE COLLEGE CLASSROOM THROUGH MEMORY SYSTEMS

"Memory is the mother of all wisdom" (Aeschylus), and as such it is the most valuable tool a student has in his or her possession. It is not difficult to grasp how learning and memory are linked. Learning is the acquisition of knowledge, while memory is the expression of acquired knowledge.

Learning and memory are the function of the brain that most people take for granted. Both learning and memory are processes rather than structures, meaning that they cannot be located in a specific part of the brain; however, they are very effective instruments in how humans learn, store, and retrieve information. One of LEP's key learning features is that it takes into account how the students' mind is organized and uses it as a tool for authentic and effective learning and memory retention of information learned. It doesn't matter what the information is and what discipline it arrives from; with LEP all information is treated equally and processed in the same way. LEP achieves success in moving the information from short- to long-term memory because it shifts the mindset of students from "content absorption" to "content connection," thereby activating students' various memory processes, which trigger the mind to access the existing information and offers effortless memory retrieval of information when needed through personalized memory hacks.

New learning is achieved by tapping into students' stored memories. The process begins when information is absorbed by the student. Because LEP learning relies heavily on existing memories to learn new information, basic memory systems will be reviewed in this chapter as a backdrop to LEP learning and memory retention processes.

Content absorption begins in sensory memory and moves to short-term memory. Students reviewing and memorizing information, a method on which most students rely to get through exams, may assist in remembering the information learned for the short-term or a specific period of time, but content connection that occurs in the long-term memory expands existing memories to form a new understanding of the concepts under study in a way that students feel personally and often emotionally connected to the subject matter. The material learned by personal connection is easier to recall later because it is reinforced through meaning and interpretation of the concept learned in a uniquely personal way. Creating a specific memory hack to recall the information later will also significantly increase information retrieval.

THE THREE MEMORY SYSTEMS OF LIVED EXPERIENCES

Memory is the capacity for storing and retrieving information and the best resource available for learning. The three memory systems that guide all human life are sensory (senses related), short-term (working) and long-term (categorized, and storage). The mind is organized so that sensory memory stores incoming information for a very brief time before it moves into short-term memory where it is held for seconds to minutes before transferred long-term memory. Researchers consider short-term memory working memory rather than just temporary storage space because short-term memory is an active working system. Long-term memory possesses unlimited capacity and is key in the LEP teaching and learning methods.

Long-term memory includes explicit (conscious) declarative memories consisting of episodic and semantic memories that operate within lived experiences and the events realm. Nondeclarative implicit (unconscious) memories consist of procedural memories, which focus on elements such as skills and tasks. The three memory systems are very much dependent on one another and play a pivotal role in learning because memory is essential for understanding the world around us and to storing information for retrieval purposes. The strength and storage of the memory depends on the strength of the memory that the LEP involves. The stronger the memory, and the greater the importance of new information, the quicker the recall.

Memory systems are intricate and complex in design, but in brief, the process of remembering information involves three general steps: encoding (perceiving), storing (maintaining), and retrieving (accessing when needed). Since senses are linked to the central nervous system, which is comprised of the spinal cord and brain, during every moment of a human beings' life, sensory information is being taken in by sensory memory. Thus, sensory memory is the starting point, which creates an LEP and starts the process of learning and memory retention (see figure 3.1).

LEP and Sensory Memory

The process of learning and memory begins with sensory memory. Sensory memory assists students to absorb new information and is a buffer for stimuli generated by the five senses of sight, hearing, smell, taste, and touch. This perception or absorption is often out of cognitive control and an automatic response, which allows the person freedom to either detect the stimuli (lived experience) or ignore it. If ignored, the stimulus immediately disappears from the mind. If detected, the stimulus is allowed entry into sensory memory and begins the LEP process. Even though this process does not require any conscious control, it does play an important role in storing information temporarily in the short-term (working) memory and with appropriate coding transference of new information to the long-term memory.

Sensory memory is the first line of an imprint and allows for the information to make its way into the consciousness and temporarily rest in short-term (working) memory. To reinforce sensory memory when teaching through LEP, sensory memory should be emphasized in combined ways. For example, during lectures the information should be imparted through a combination of ways such as auditory effects, visual aids, or props, such as pictures, images/visuals, colors, symbols, or personal examples of a lived experience in which to frame to concept(s). This combined exposure to new information from various sensory perceptions will reach students with varied learning abilities, and greatly assist them in understanding the concept. Moreover, an increased pool of lived experiences to choose from

Figure 3.1 LEP Memory Process Chart

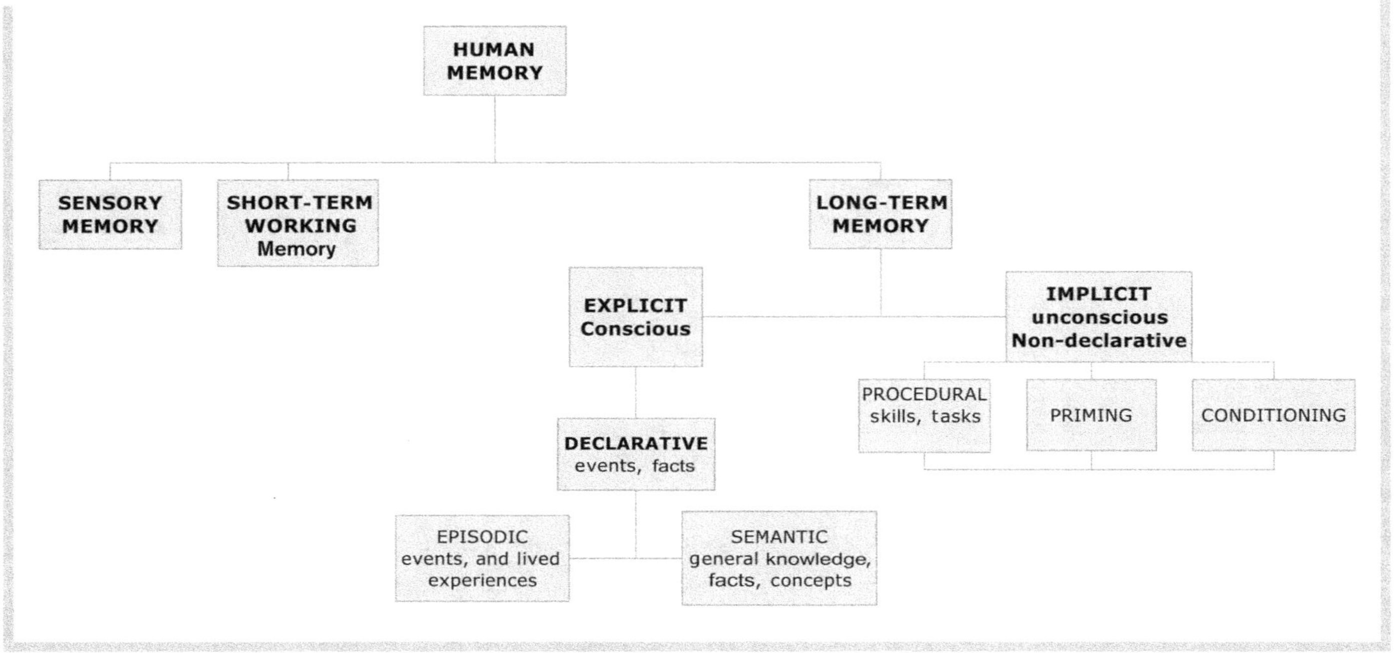

```
                          HUMAN
                          MEMORY
         ┌───────────────────┼───────────────────┐
    SENSORY          SHORT-TERM            LONG-TERM
    MEMORY           WORKING               MEMORY
                     Memory
                                    ┌──────────┴──────────┐
                                EXPLICIT              IMPLICIT
                                Conscious             unconscious
                                                      Non-declarative
                                    │              ┌───────┼────────┐
                              DECLARATIVE      PROCEDURAL PRIMING CONDITIONING
                              events, facts    skills, tasks
                              ┌─────┴─────┐
                          EPISODIC      SEMANTIC
                          events, and   general knowledge,
                          lived         facts, concepts
                          experiences
```

CHAPTER THREE MEMORY SYSTEMS

that can be related to better link or can explain the material under study will give students many ideas as to how the concept(s) can work in their own life. Other influences of the educator that can effect student learning are tactics such as raising the tone of voice to emphasize important facts, associating information imparted with smell, using touch examples, or using mind-mapping activities specifically designed to capture sensory memories, will also significantly aid in the acquisition and encoding of new information.

Reinforcing information taught through sensory props, personal meaning, or personal examples will successfully move the information from sensory memory to the next step of memory processing to short-term (working) memory, which allows students to work with information until it is moved into the long-term memory through encoding. The longer the students work with new information, the better the chances that the information will be transferred to long-term memory. One sense, or a combination of senses, may bring various perceptions or interpretations of the new information and expand on the content definition and its applications in a number of ways. Sensory systems may bring about existing memories of our favorite food, place, or a smell of a perfume or cologne that brings back a memory of a significant person, a lesson, an experiment worked on, an old learning, or a perception of something or any other happening. Symbols, situations, occasions, or events or feeling of them that can be even remotely connected to the concept under study can be used to expand understanding and increase the possibility of long-term memory retention of the new knowledge.

LEP teaching and learning deliberately arouse sensory processes so that personal memories pop up and trigger moments of the students' life so that they can be connected to new information and form new learning. If one sense is stimulated to evoke a memory, other senses may follow suit and trigger additional memories that can further explain and expand the application of the concept(s). LEP teaching and learning should utilize as many sensory memory (touch, sight, smell, hear, and taste) processes to learn and remember information as possible. This is especially important at the introduction of new information because encoding is responsible for creating a new memory.

The more personal or interesting the new information is during the encoding process, the greater the chance of it being categorized and moved into long-term memory. Through sensory information, encoding allows new information to be converted to a construct and moved from short-term to long-term memory and stored in the brain to be available for later recall. The sensory input a person receives must be changed into a construct so that it may be understood enough to be categorized and stored.

LEP and Short-Term Memory

Short-term memory absorbs and keeps a short amount of information in the active and readily available state for a short amount of time. The duration of information in short-term memory is generally about 15–30 seconds, typically no more than a minute before the information is either amalgamated into long-term memory (Miller, 1956) or lost (forgotten). Short-term memory cannot be stored for later use but must be worked with immediately even as new information is surfacing that must be integrated. Information can be retained longer if repetition is involved, a process known as rehearsal. However, for the most part short-term memory equals to what the individual notices, or is cognizant of, at any given instant, which is the individual's conscious experience, the LEP, and LEP moment(s).

Short-term memory, as sensory memory, operates mostly in the content absorption state, whereas long-term memory offers content connection to the information, where learning occurs. Learning happens when information is transferred from short-term to long-term memory and is available to be retrieved and used. However, all states are equally important to initiate and achieve learning and memory retention because without the sensory and short-term memory focus on content absorption, it would not be possible to achieve personal content connection and long-term memory retention.

LEP and Long-Term Memory

Learning occurs when information is transferred to long-term memory and is available to be retrieved and used. Long-term memory refers to the infinite storage of information in a human brain and is largely outside of people's daily awareness. It is the final stage in memory providing lasting retention of all our lived experiences, information, and skills.

Long-term memories may exist in some of the same places and categories in the brain, but they are not of equal strength. Stronger memories, or memories that are more important, elicit stronger feelings and are easier to recall than memories that were either unimportant or insignificant. In some cases, people misremember, fabricate, or remember things to their advantage. Moreover, often individuals fill in missing "gaps" in information with their version of events.

Other times, older memories can interfere with the formation of new ones, rendering the old memories questionable as to what really happened. However, with LEP it is of no consequence what the validity of the "truth" is; the focus is on connecting to information that explains or defines the concept(s) and expands its understanding and applications. The memory of the raw or altered experience can easily be used to frame new understanding of the concept, provided it is in-line with its authentic academic definition. LEP also assists in retrieval because content connection allows students to relearn rather than learn new information by expanding on existing knowledge; new information once formed is much easier to remember.

LEP and Explicit (Declarative) Memories

Long-term memory within the human memory systems also includes two key processes: explicit (conscious) memories and implicit (unconscious) memories. The explicit declarative memory system holds what can be expressed or articulated by the learners. It includes episodic (events and lived experiences) and semantic (general factual knowledge) memories, which are both of particular interest to the LEP teaching method model.

Explicit memories register the lived experience. The most significant form of explicit memory for subjective experience is the episodic memory (Solms & Turnbull, 2002). Solms and Turnbull (2002) noted that this type of memory involves the integration of the two avenues of experience. The first is the subjected state from the inner processes such as perceptions; this is coupled with the second state of externally sensed events through the sensory system, smell, sight, or any other sensory ability.

Since LEP focuses on learning through lived experience, episodic memories are of monumental importance to stimulate the brain to integrate new information with new material. Solms and Turnbull (2002) contend that the subjective experiences of an individual, itself initially unconscious, and linked with memory traces of external situations, comprise the episodic memory and their lived experience. According to Solms and Turnbull (2002, p. 161), "Experiences are not mere traces of past stimuli. Experiences have to be lived. It is the reliving of an event as an 'experience' ('I remember . . .') that necessarily renders it conscious." Since students tap into the conscious mind when learning new information, a personal connection with the material assists in engaging them emotionally, which increases long-term memory retention.

Episodic memories record all lived experiences from which the individual can reconstruct the actual occurrences at any point in life. Episodic memories are the memories of autobiographical data that include times, places, situations, and events and involve the inclusion of personal meaning, interpretations, feelings, and emotions relating to the experience, as a part of the memory. Since many individuals make decisions based on how they feel, rather than what they know, episodic memories subconsciously play a strategic role in behavior and are an important part in new learning and retaining learned information for future use. Deliberate strategies to employ episodic learning in explaining concepts, especially through the use of feelings when appropriate and applicable, should be made by educators to reinforce content in long-term memory.

Explicit memories require conscious thought. One of the benefits of using LEP's inquisitive reflection, which uses explicit memories in the classroom, is that it significantly increases students' critical thinking skills. Students inquisitively reflect (think deeply and inquiringly) about the new information they are learning and its application using explicit cognitions and first-person self-reference. Reflective memory through the probing of LEP's inquisitive reflection leads to greater understanding of the information being learned, self-insight, and self-growth. It also presents students with an opportunity to expand their knowledge base with easier comprehension of the information being learned because it is always easier to understand something when it can be linked to existing memories, existing framing.

When using explicit memories to learn and remember information, students should be free to explore and be creative in their content connections. Even simple things like memories of people's faces, music that was playing, the smell of a Christmas tree, might all be a part of a memory of an evening with family, but independently just the smell of the tree, or a particular song that might have been playing that night, will bring back that memory. Any memory that is significant enough to tie to the content is appropriate, and all lived experiences that are relevant to the new information should be used to tap into these memories. Strong LEP connection to the new information being learned will reframe the content into a more personal connection for the student seen through their own unique lens, which will allow for more solid memory retention of information and an easier retrieval of the stored information.

Semantic memories refer to a part of the long-term memory that processes concepts that were not drawn from personal lived experiences. They are linked to everyday recollections, processed ideas, and concepts that include a general knowledge of facts, such as knowing the functions of items, or names of colors, or that Washington, D.C., is the Capital of the United States. Semantic memory includes all common knowledge and general world knowledge that people accumulate over their lifetime.

The combination of episodic and semantic memories gives human beings an overall picture of their lived experience. This information can be used for framing of new information as it comes in to be used for current and future learning. For example, knowing that a living Christmas tree is green is an example of semantic memory; recalling what happened when you went to buy that green Christmas tree is an episodic memory. Thus, both episodic and semantic memories are important and serve humans in the memory process, and can be used for new learning and increased memory retention of the learned material.

LEP teaching methods use the combination of episodic and semantic memories to reinforce new information through LEP's inquisitive reflection. LEP's inquisitive reflection is effective when probing episodic memories but is also exceptionally skilled at placing a conscious focus on semantic memories to connect to the content being learned. This approach to learning engages the students' brains as they connect the new information to their personal experiences and narratives in their own life to create an expanded understanding of what they are learning. This interactive student engagement increases the ability of the students to encode new information with greater ease into their long-term memory and increases the ability to recall it later because of the personal connection to the new information.

LEP and Implicit (Nondeclarative) Memories

Implicit/nondeclarative memories are unconscious and include, among others, procedural memories, such as priming and conditioning (discussed in Chapter 5). Implicit memory includes elements that people don't purposely remember because it is a product of indirect processes, meaning that implicit memories are enabled by previous cognitive experiences. Implicit memories hold implicit learning of any motor skill or cognitive activity and stand in contrast to explicit memory because it is an unconscious process. However, implicit memory is important in the LEP teaching paradigm because it has a direct effect on human beings' skills and learned behaviors and can be used as a valuable tool in new learning and memory retention.

Procedural Memories

Procedural memories usually involve unconscious procedures and include the knowledge of motor skills like riding a bike, playing a piano, tying a shoe, and so on. Procedures or processes that are frequently repeated are stored in the cerebellum for easy access and are used frequently in people's life without their conscious effort. The LEP teaching methods can tap into procedural memories and use them to expand concept understanding by connecting information that needs to be learned (if appropriate) to procedural information that is already stored in the students' brain.

There are various ways and hands-on techniques that can be used to help students access procedural memory routes to learn and retain new information. Examples by the educator top the list. Giving students a peek into how to tap into their procedural memories as they relate to the content they are teaching can often help explain the concept under study uniquely to each student for a deeper understanding and application. Thus, it can be used by educators as an effective learning tool in the classroom and open up discussions that vastly add to the information already presented.

Priming

Priming is the introduction of new information before the lesson begins in a way that students will recognize the information later. It hinges on the premise that by giving a person a point of reference, they are more likely to be directed and think from and toward that point, unlike framing, which has to do with how the content is presented and the way it can operate in the world. Priming is an interesting psychological phenomenon and often involves an unconscious memory of a past experience that changes a perception of a current understanding, which brings new understanding and faster recollection of the memory in the future. For example, if during priming, an individual sees the word "green," they will be slightly faster to recognize the words "grass" as the lesson progresses. If a woman has learned that she is pregnant, she may start seeing babies everywhere. Seeing babies everywhere is the response to the priming of the recent lived experience of finding out about the pregnancy. If a student had just seen a movie on historic buildings, they are much more likely to notice related stimuli, such as historic buildings, on the way home from class, which can be associated to the concepts learned that day and even used as a memory hack to remember the information later.

Thus, priming is the mechanism that activates representations and knowledge structures of an experience (point of reference) that influences the response with increased reaction time to the later stimulus. Priming is unconscious and often includes emotional memory, such as having intense feelings about things even when one cannot remember the situation or knowing why they feel like they do. Emotions can be a very effective tool for priming purposes if they can be directly related to the topic under study.

In learning, when introducing new concepts, students' brains are tuned in to what is being taught. Thus, priming is important in LEP teaching and learning because this preview of exposure will assist students to better understand the information when presented in full during the lesson or lecture. Promoting priming in the classroom in sensory or subliminal forms, or through various student learning abilities or lived experience contexts yours or the students' yields quicker understanding of content, and better memory retention of learned information.

The students don't feel priming happening, but the educators know and are actively engaging the students' brain. It only makes sense to prime our students for a few minutes for the lesson at hand at every meet so that they are ready and in the right frame of mind to absorb and connect with the new information in a personal way. Helping students prime their brains for learning through any stimulus appropriate to the lesson of the day, in personal ways before delving into the actual concept, can be of great benefit to the students' learning process and can assist in significant memory retention of information learned later.

Previews of what is to come in the lesson plan is always hugely beneficial to student learning and memory retention and should be practiced regularly by educators. Examples of priming can include various thoughts expressed to students on the subject matter relating to how the educator personally perceives the topic. Subliminal and stimulating messages, any type of sensory motivators, such as reviewing worksheets or showing a class a related image or two of the content that is being introduced, and why it is personally important to them can also be shared in a quick way to prime the students to the topic they are about to delve into. Sharing a personal connection to the material about to be presented also gives students a point of reference and an opportunity to connect their own lived experiences to their understanding of the material as they are learning.

Some preparation to priming students in the classroom to new topics is necessary to prepare their minds for the new information in an optimal manner. Each discipline may call for different types of preparation or methods; thus, educators must always consider the subject matter and the priming delivery format to ensure the best content memory priming results. Asking questions such as "How is the student's mind to absorb this new information so they can connect to it personally? What is the best priming delivery approach? Will priming occur through an image, a video, a lived personal experience, or a discussion?" will assist the educator to plan out the priming methods for each lesson plan. Priming the brain for the specific content that will be presented in class presents educators with enormous opportunities to set the stage for increased understanding, engagement, and long-term memory retention of the material being learned.

Framing

New information is easier to understand and remember when it is framed. Framing gives students the information they need to maximize the potential learning that will follow because it focuses on how the information is presented, and not just offering a point of reference, as in the priming process. In framing, the educator provides a framework for the learning about to take place by offering personal examples of how he or she connects to the content, and ways the students can connect to the content, allowing students to be better prepared to connect to the topic and search for examples of their own as the lesson progresses.

Framing is a feature of our brain's structural design mechanisms. Experienced educators know how important framing is when introducing new information to students. Human minds react to the context in which something is embedded and try to find patterns or existing blue prints in the memory systems to create meaning. The introduction of the framework structure of the concept better prepares students for new information and assists their short-term memory retention.

LEP framing differs from the "traditional framing of concepts" because it links unique personal information to provide the structural framework of the concept under study, and not just random examples students may or may not associate with. Moreover, it uses the framework process as a note-taking technique. This allows for the understanding of content's application and creates visual snapshot representation through personal mind maps designed by the students themselves as they frame information in their minds to understand its meaning and applications.

Framing of concepts is also an important step in the memory-encoding process. Once framed, the information moves from short-term to long-term memory through the encoding process. LEP encoding techniques, when moving information from short-term memory to long-term memory, must relate new concepts being learned (content absorption) to ones that the student is already familiar with (content connection) through LEP's inquisitive reflection. If on the encoding journey through the memory systems, the information does not elicit interest on the students' part; for example, if the students find the lecture or presentation boring, they feel detached from the material being taught, or don't really understand the concepts as explained, appropriate framing has failed, and the encoding has a very limited effect on learning and long-term memory retention.

Students' engagement and interest in the information learned and their ability to frame the incoming information so that they can make sense of it play a key role in the strength and effectiveness of the encoding process because even though parts of the brain like Broca's area (related to the production of speech) and Wernicke's area (sensory area, which assists in understanding speech and using correct words for expression) will be activated, the information mainly will be processed in the language part of the brain to decode the words into general meaning, without any real lasting memory, and most likely will be forgotten. Personal examples either from the educators' own life, the student, or the offering of the other students that connect to the content learned will significantly assist in the encoding of information from short-term to long-term memory. This process will expand understanding and increase memory retention of the subject matter not only in the students who shared the information, but in the class as a whole.

Time and attention are crucial in short-term (working) memory; the more attention and mental effort is placed on the stimuli at the introduction of the framing process, the easier the encoding process into long-term memory will be. During the encoding process from short-term memory to long-term memory, the focus is to connect new information to the student's lived experience in a common way, and the best way is to begin with framing. If the students can connect information being learned with an event, a fact, a place, a person, a thing, a feeling, a situation, or any significant memory that exists within them, and can frame if for their understanding, which will give the information personal meaning, they can access that information later through a memory hack, which will trigger the information when they need it.

Even though on the onset traditional and LEP framing of content may appear similar, the two include different ideologies. In a typical college classroom, the educator will most likely review the textbook definitions through a lecture combined with a PowerPoint and will provide additional applications relative to the concept but in a manner that applies mostly to the world at large. Thus, in the traditional scenario the format in which note taking takes place is left largely to the student. LEP framing is because it insists that notes are taken using visuals in a mind mapping manner, and include personal informal for memory retrieval purposes. LEP framing is different because it insists that notes are taken using visuals in a mind mapping manner, and include personal informal for memory retrieval purposes. LEP framing is interactive and offers various applications as both the educator and students work with the same academic (textual) information, but in addition, they frame the concept structurally and provide examples of a personal nature to demonstrate the understanding and application of what they are learning. All notes are recorded through the visual framing process.

LEP framing stresses an ideology of a hands-on, personal approach to be included in all lesson plans, with each concept learned framed in a manner that each student can understand. Educators must demonstrate to students how to frame concepts and include personal information relative to the concept by either using white/black/board or through prepared LEP content framing practice worksheets. When using framing practice sheets, students become involved in active participation which signals to the brain that the material is important to consider.

Learning new content using personal information further reiterates that message, but in order for the message to be effective, educators must demonstrate the best way to frame the concepts, even if it is a simple board exercise. As a quick example, the educator should write the concept in the center, or at the base of a white board or blackboard, put a circle around it, and start branching out and fill in more details that fit the concept by using both textual and structural information, showing its various connections and application.

Another quick and effective way to illustrate concept framing to students is the use of a flow chart to show how information could be linked. The framework should include both textual and structural links and personal association and applications to the concepts and should be completed with some type of an image, which can assist as a memory hack to retrieve the information later. LEP assessments have included the findings that students catch on very quickly and can create their own LEP mind maps in which to frame new information in a personal way almost from the onset of the course, but to most students demonstrations and illustrations by educators of how to start the framing process is necessary.

There are various ways educators can impart information through LEP framing diagrams. Many LEP educators provide preset LEP framing worksheets that match the lesson plans with the content outlined in one visual snapshot offering both textual and structural interpretations and include examples of memory hacks to retain the information. Other LEP educators require students to modify and fill in their personal connections to the subject matter and include a memory hack of how they will remember the information in an assignment format. Still others prefer the LEP blank slate framing, with only the main concept filled in, and have the student create their own LEP framing for the content they are learning uninhibited by any suggestions of how the content should be organized or what type of memory hack they should use.

Once all students understand the LEP framing process, students should be reminded to take notes by using framing with any visual processes such as simple mind mapping, tree branch style, or flow chart method to understand and remember the content for the duration of the course and beyond. LEP framing process is a highly effective tool for note taking because it visually organizes information at a glance and allows students to add their personal information in a way that easily explains the content under study. Even students who may have decided that participating in note taking was not necessary, and just sat silently disinterested until the class was over, will find framing new information engaging, which will motivate them to pay attention, identify with, and remember the new information.

Notes without personal connections or association to the subject matter are just words on paper and are not likely to be retained for later use, such as on tests. The students who were engaged enough to take notes usually in the traditional linear way of writing down random information or verbatim, which usually overshadowed important information, and others who managed to organize their notes but did so without any real connection to what they were learning, in the end, were all left in the same space. They were left without true understanding or connection to the information they were learning and as a result could not apply the information. Collecting and recording information randomly without organizing and categorizing often will result in pages and pages of notes where important information may be lost because of the quantity of irrelevant information. However, with LEP framing students can easily spot and record critical information in a shortened form visually and have a complete organized overview of the concepts at a glance.

Educators must illustrate concept framing in the courses they teach, and students must be encouraged to frame new information for their understanding so that authentic learning and increased memory retention can occur. Traditional learning turns into memorization very quickly if students are not engaged and do not understand the information. Framing new information as part of a regular lesson plan and encouraging students to work with and take notes through the framing process broadens the scope of students' understanding and how the concepts being taught personally apply to them, which leads to long-term memory retention of the material learned.

CHAPTER FOUR

LEP Memory Trigger Categories

LEP Sensory Memory Trigger Categories
Categorizing Triggers by Senses
See/Visual
Smell
Taste
Hear
Touch

LEP MEMORY TRIGGERS

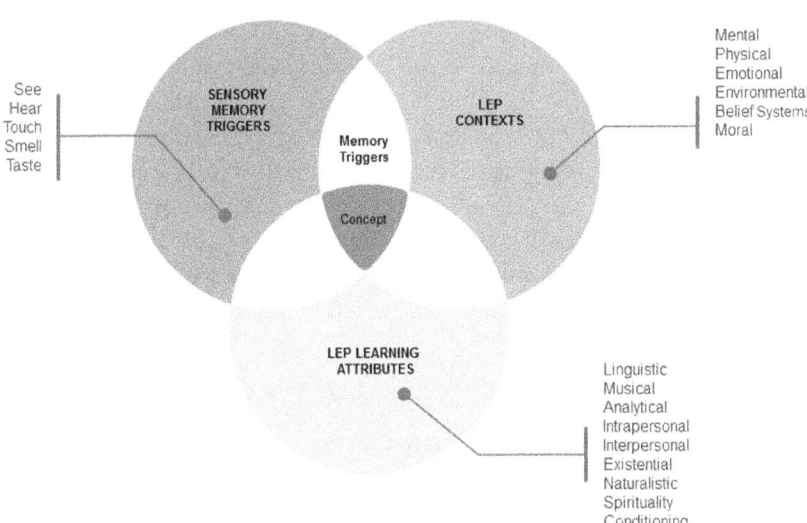

LEP MEMORY TRIGGER CATEGORIES

Memories are categorized in the brain and lay dormant until they are summoned or are triggered by memory cues. The three memory trigger categories used for reactivation in LEP teaching and learning include (1) LEP Sensory Memory (2) LEP Learning Attributes, and (3) LEP Contexts. Others could and should be added by the educator to suit the needs of the students and the course.

Reactivation is the first step in memory retrieval and a vital starting point for triggered memories to make connections with new information. Reactivation is central to LEP learning because memory is brought from an inactive to an active state by a trigger that is associated with the concept under study and made available for current use and future learning. But in LEP, which memory trigger category will be reactivated depends on the concept itself, sensory perceptions, innate learning abilities, or the person's lived experiences.

By asking questions, what does this concept or information remind me of? How can I link it with what I already know? In what way can I connect with this information? What strikes me first when I hear it? Do I have any existing feelings about it? How can I use my imagination to frame this concept so that I can understand it? Students can frame new information within their current frame of understanding for clearer comprehension and concept application. When new information is presented, the students' minds should be programmed to immediately search for triggers to reactivate existing knowledge that will help to inform, frame, and form the new learning.

Once associated, the information accommodates new learning in a personally unique way, and now is primed to be recalled later when needed. Students must be encouraged to use the information that was triggered relative to the concept to expand its definitions and applications in as many ways as possible because viewing a concept from various vantage points opens new avenues for expanded or varied definitions, which will assist in offering students options in which to apply the information. The additional time and effort students spent on the concepts will vastly assist in long-term memory retention and retrieval of information when needed.

According to Gisquet-Verrier and Ricco (2012), memory reactivation has two goals: (1) to enhance the accessibility of the target memory and (2) to make the memory malleable. Malleable is having the capability of change, of shaping something into something else without breaking the original intent. LEP is aligned with this process, as it takes existing knowledge and, by adding the new concept under study, builds upon that knowledge, creating new wisdom.

The old wisdom is not lost; it has now been expanded, made malleable, with new definition(s) and connection(s) to personal application(s). Gisquet-Verrier and Ricco (2012) indicate that reactivation generates a transient state during which the content of the memory is easily accessible and can be modified and/or updated. The authors further propose that memory reactivation is considered "in its own right," and not merely as the preliminary stage of retrieval or reconsolidation, but as a distinct stage of memory processing that plays a fundamental role with respect to preexisting memories (Gisquet-Verrier & Ricco, 2012).

Reactivation is generated by cues that are either external or self-generated and occur in two general conditions (Gisquet-Verrier & Ricco, 2012). First, reactivation is required for retrieval and for every operation that enlarges or modifies the previous knowledge. Second, reactivation may also occur when subjects are simply re-exposed to cues or reminder stimuli specific to a particular episode (Gisquet-Verrier & Ricco, 2012). LEP can be seen as a cue-induced learning process because the students consciously target memories and cue the brain to connect to the concept to frame their understanding of new information. Additionally, with LEP students do not have to specifically rely on cue-induced triggers but may also take advantage of spontaneous memory cues, which can easily trigger existing memories of information students may find useful to assist in the current learning.

Although in most cases, sensory memory is the first line of perception and sensation, memory can be triggered from any other category such as learning abilities/attributes or lived experiences (Figure 4.1). Sensory triggers processed through sensory memory of vision/seeing, aural/hearing, taste, smell, and touch trigger the most and varied memories that relate to the new information and can be used for new learning. The learning attributes category is focused on categorizing triggers by the strongest innate learning attribute that each student uniquely possesses, such as being musically inclined, naturalistic, interpersonal, intrapersonal, linguistic, logical existential, or soul (holistic) motivated. Lastly, the LEP Contexts categorizes triggers by personal meaning and association through the following contexts: biological, emotional, environmental, mental, moral, and spiritual. (A quick overview of how each of the trigger categories may work with a concept is demonstrated through the example of the concept "ego" in Activity 7).

LEP SENSORY MEMORY TRIGGER CATEGORIES

The learning process begins with sensory memory. Sensory memory is the perception of hearing, sight, smell, taste, and touch. Sensory memory allows all living beings to sense information around them. This is how human beings learn, but as with

Figure 4.1 LEP Sensory Trigger Categories

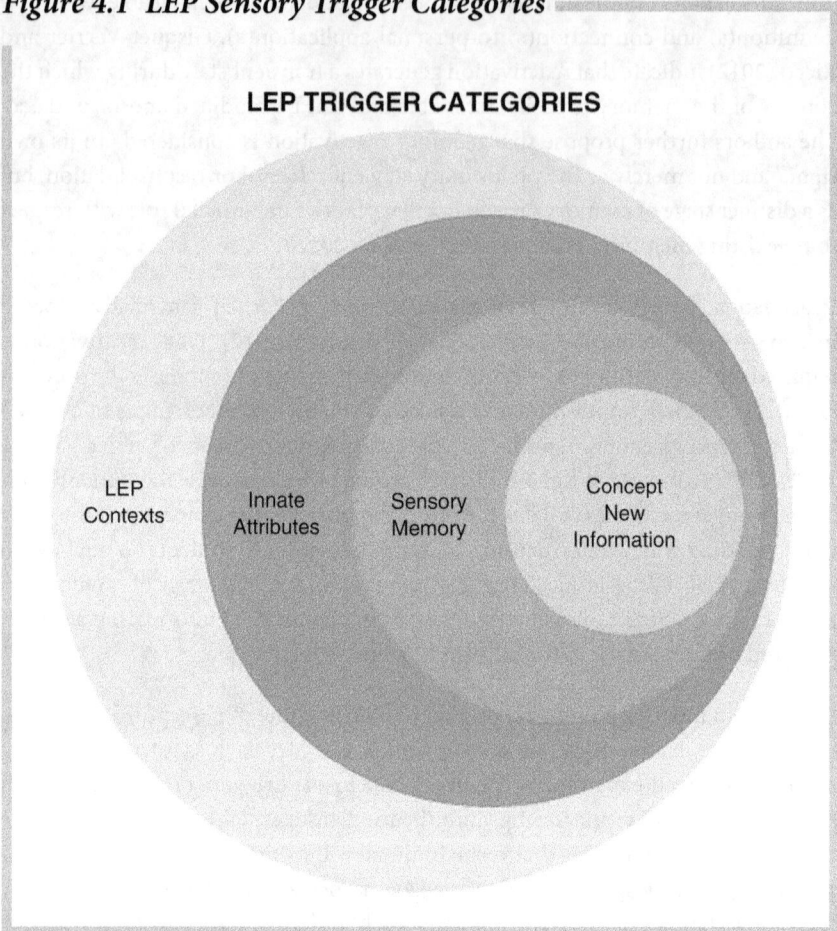

everything else, people have choices; they can either detect it and decide if it could be used, or ignore it, whereby it disappears from the mind.

LEP sensory triggers include the five commonly recognized senses of vision, hearing, touch, taste, and smell and are a vital resource in LEP learning and memory retention. Choosing a trigger sense or a combination of senses that will search, find, and expand the understanding of the concept under study, as well as create a memory hack to retrieve the information when needed, will considerably increase the comprehension of the material under study and significantly increase the possibility of long-term retention. Using the senses to trigger experiences from the past to learn new knowledge strengthens critical thinking skills and can be a very empowering exercise, as often students see patterns in themselves and learn not only about the concept under study, and their applications, but how their brain perceives and processes information.

Sensory memory is the first line of an imprint and allows for the information to make its way into the consciousness and temporarily rest in short-term/working memory. This perception or awareness of the senses often is out of cognitive control and is an automatic response, which allows the person freedom to either detect the stimuli or ignore it. If ignored, the stimulus disappears from the mind. If detected, the stimulus enters the sensory memory and begins the LEP process. Even though this process does not require any conscious control, it does play an important role in storing information in short-term/working memory and eventually long-term memory. People's senses work collectively to provide a complete picture of human lived experiences. Many of these come from memories that were compartmentalized by the students using their sensory memories; thus, these same sensory memories can be triggered when students need to frame new information for understanding.

The human lived experience begins with sensory memory and is the initial recording of information that passes through the senses in student learning and memory retention. In LEP students use the five senses as primary methods to learn new knowledge, understand the material and their world, and gain a complete picture of their experiences. The combination of these factors will now be used to understand new information and remember it long term in a personal way. To ensure that all students have the opportunity to use their strongest innate sense (visual, taste, touch, hearing, smell) to link to their prior memories to expand their understanding of new information, and to accommodate all learners, educators must stress the importance of consciously using the senses to link to and frame new information.

Educators should further assist students in the sensory process through the use of additional resources in class, and online in the form of uploaded supplemental materials and any other tangible means to stimulate the students' senses. Props, such as pictures, images/visuals, colors, symbols, and so on, to assist in lecture, whether in class or uploaded as a video combined with the auditory effects of the instructor, such as a raised tone of voice to emphasize important facts, are very beneficial in reinforcing new information in memory. Using music, any meaningful sounds, using touch examples, or the use of LEP memory trigger activities specifically designed to capture sensory memories will significantly aid in framing and understanding new information and its applications.

The students should be reminded to use their senses to trigger memories and should have access to LEP sensory activity worksheets to aid them in this endeavor as an after-the-lesson exercise, or when taking notes during lecture or other times, as appropriate. Completing sensory sheets as relative to the concept allows students to trigger existing information in their brains and change the new information into a meaningful construct which assists them to make sense of the information so that they can understand and apply it. Through sensory information and/or meaningful information, encoding allows new information to be converted to a construct so that a student can now understand and accommodate the new knowledge, which will be compartmentalized and stored in the student's brain and available to be retrieved when needed.

Sensory memory is one of the most powerful tools in learning because with every breath that people take, stimuli from the environment is continuously being perceived as sensory images in the brain and, if detected, is processed to create memories. Each sensation is stored in its own category of sight, smell, taste, hear, or touch and in its own section of the brain and, if detected and transferred from short-term to long-term memory, the information may be retrieved with ease through LEP sensory personal memory hacks (see Chapter 7). Students of all ages, when assessed in the way they learn best, indicated that they not only understand but also remember information long-term if it can be connected to personal meaningful experiences relative to them. Thus, educators should spend even a brief amount of time bringing awareness of the processes of sensory information on student learning and memory retention either in class through a discussion or uploaded video for online students and allow them to become acquainted with the process. Knowing how information is transferred within them, will help them to identify the most preferred way they process information which will assist them in current and future learning.

CATEGORIZING TRIGGERS BY SENSES

See/Visual

Visual triggers are very important in the retrieval of learned information process not only because retrieving information is a necessary part of life and human existence, but also so that new learning can occur. Visual, which includes the spatial learning attribute, is the primary way most students learn. The part of the brain that processes visual images is the largest; thus, many researchers equate it with the reason that it is easier for people to remember something they have seen, rather than read. Once triggered, existing memories of visual interpretations give students the opportunity to draw meaningful units from their experiences and associate themselves with the concepts they are learning in a very personal way. This personal connection and visual application of the concept to the student's life greatly increase their understanding and memory retention of information.

Visual-spatial attributes allow students the capacity to think in images and pictures and visualize information accurately and abstractly. Visual students should work with information using pictures, images, and so on because in them a picture can trigger a buried memory and recall a precise moment in time much more rapidly than words. Words are abstract and challenging for the brain to retain for visual students, whereas visuals are much more engaging and easier to remember. In general, it is much harder to remember what was written at what point in time, but much easier to remember things that were seen, and often can be visualized years later, especially if the experiences were even remotely personal in nature.

Numerous studies have confirmed the power of visual imaginary in learning and memory retention. Visual stimulus is not only the most effective way students learn and remember the information, but the new information remains retrievable for some time after its contact to the stimulus because the characteristics persist, offering the possibility, at least, for some of the information to be retained and retrieved at a later time. Using imagery to learn and remember is extremely popular among students and effective because it does not exert a lot of effort in committing images to memory, yet visuals maximize learning and long-term memory retention. Most educators know this and rely on visual learning and use overheads, PowerPoints, black/white boards, pictures, images, graphs, maps, and many other visual items like color to entice and engage students in the material. LEP educators use all of the traditional visual methods mentioned but they also place a great deal of emphasis on creative visualization and imagination, as mental imagery visual tools to remember information.

Anything meaningful that can represent a visual memory of the experience real or imagined relative to what the students are learning and need to remember can be used as a tool for new learning. Visual learners can, in great detail, visualize how the new information fits into their existing knowledge base and how it relates to them personally. This innate attribute should be stressed by the educator to visual students so that they can be made aware of how they can use visual learning consciously as a tool to frame new information for their understanding. Since visual students love recreating memories that are very detailed in visual acuity and often use vivid colors, textures, and so on, they should be encouraged to make their memories come alive using vivid expressions frequently. Students should be inspired to freely use visual experiences to relate to the concepts while considering its applications to themselves or the world at large.

Free play through the imagination is strongly encouraged when students are beginning to work with LEP visual memory triggers. The more students play the more they are engaged and the longer they will work with the information. The more they work with information, their knowledge base expands. To connect new information to the existing knowledge, students should find examples of questions they should ask themselves to help them link with their sensory memories relative to the subject at hand. Did the students see themselves or someone else have an experience? Did they see an image, or make an observation about something or someone that was similar to the concept under study?

Any and all images are encouraged during playtime as the more vivid and elaborate the memory, the more perceptual lenses can be directed at the concept for the best interpretation and framework. Branching out and having choices with various images students can connect to explain the subject matter will significantly increase their understanding and application of the concepts. To boost visual learning, educators can have students draw or create pictures of any experience that will help to increase the understanding of the concept under study.

Visual learners excel at using creative visualization as a trigger tool to retrieve memories that relate to the framing and understanding of concepts they are learning. Visual learners have an unusual ability to tap deeply into their creative visualizations, into that part of the brain that processes visual images and categorizes them into a particular field of understanding, which expands the students' frame of interpretations and increases the ability to remember the new information. Visual learners usually have a great imagination, which can assist in retrieving information from long-term memory that can be connected to new information fairly easily.

Educators should encourage all students to use their creative visualization skills as a tool when they are learning. Visual learners, especially, excel at creative visualization and should find working with visual triggers to retrieve information relative to the concept they are learning beneficial. Additionally, generating visual mental imagery of the concept relative to what is already known about the concept can be a very purposeful exercise in the transformation of the concepts, its definitions, and application to form new learning. It also assists in better memory retention of the learned information because of the personal association and the understanding of the associated feelings, which always help in long-term memory of information.

If students are unaware of how to use creative visualization, they should be instructed in basic ways keeping in mind that directions should be clear and simple, such as to relax and sit quietly, with some verbal suggestive cues that can be given to assist students to begin the creative visualization process. If suggesting students use verbal cues, ensure that they are short and suggestive, for example, "visualize the concept ... describe it ... remember an experience when the concept related to your life ... how can you connect the concept to the experience ... think of a time when ..." Leading cues by the educator to further instruct the student to search deeper into their memory could also be made until students are familiar enough with practice to work with it on their own."

Lastly, all learners, but in particular visual learners, are strongly encouraged to take notes using the flow chart process or at least utilize note-taking methods in diagram forms or in sketches of information so that it is visually organized. Often taking notes in this way triggers existing knowledge that students already have within themselves to help them frame incoming information and add to the notes they have already taken.

Smell

Smell can trigger responses relative to old experiences that can be used for new learning. The olfactory student learns best through the sense of smell Davis, (2007) not the institute my error! (Institute for Learning Styles, 2003); thus, smell memories are often the choice of new learning for these students. Very often when people smell a certain aroma, perfume, food, and so on, it affects them, as in some cases, memories come flooding back; some may be good, others not so good, but good or bad are just labels, all memories can be used to explain existing information, and have the capacity to integrate it with new information to form and create new meaning and new understanding of the subject matter at hand.

Marcel Proust, best known for his novel *Remembrance of Things Past*, vividly describes how smell can transport people through time to experience the past by the powerful emotions stirred by smells. Named after Proust, the "Proustian Phenomenon" suggests that distinctive smells have more power than any other sense to help us recall distant memories. Proust linked memory recall as having a strong unconscious connection to certain smells, and other research supports this finding. Although research has not firmly substantiated Proust's assumption that the phenomenon is real, research in smell and memory includes the findings that smell triggers more detailed memories than that of other senses like sound. Toffolo, Smeets, and van den Hout's (2012) research suggested that smell is a stronger trigger of detailed and arousing memories than music.

Research indicates that people subconsciously associate smells with different memories and that information is held in long-term memory ready to be triggered by the student in order to understand new information. Any smell can be traced to an experience or a memory, whether it included humans, animals, food, places, flowers, perfume, chemistry experiments, and so on, and, if applicable, can be used as a memory trigger to connect new learning to existing knowledge. Practice using smell memories with your students to better reinforce the concepts they are learning, if appropriate. A powerful illustration of the sense of smell can be demonstrated in the classroom as the smell is applied to certain concepts that will evoke memories that will explain the concept further. The sense of smell is not an undervalued sense. It has been found to be very effective in learning and long-term memory retention in many areas such as science and nursing. The more students are aware that they have sensory power memories of smell available to them, the more they can practice using the sense of smell for current and future learning.

Taste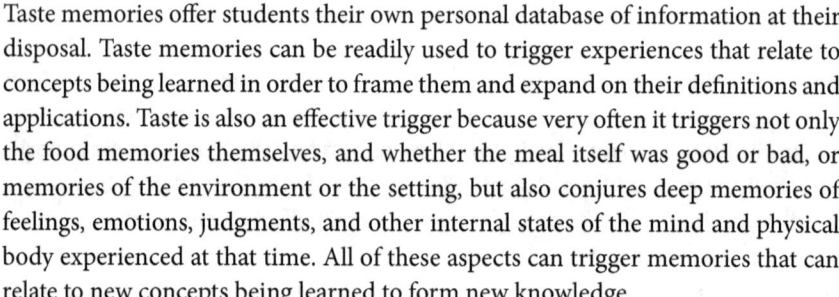

Taste memories offer students their own personal database of information at their disposal. Taste memories can be readily used to trigger experiences that relate to concepts being learned in order to frame them and expand on their definitions and applications. Taste is also an effective trigger because very often it triggers not only the food memories themselves, and whether the meal itself was good or bad, or memories of the environment or the setting, but also conjures deep memories of feelings, emotions, judgments, and other internal states of the mind and physical body experienced at that time. All of these aspects can trigger memories that can relate to new concepts being learned to form new knowledge.

Taste is the direct perception of the tongue. Taste is what is detected by the taste buds (receptor cells), which are based on the front and back of the tongue and on the sides, back, and roof of the mouth. These taste buds bind with molecules from the food or drink consumed and transmit signals to the brain. Bitter tastes are more detected toward the back of the mouth and sweet tastes at the front. Taste is connected to the involuntary nervous system and is just a bundle of different sensations that, combined with other elements, plays a part in what is perceived as taste. Attributes of taste include various elements such as the perception of the tongue, the smell, and the texture. Even temperature is important in the perception of taste, and all attributes can be used to trigger memories to frame new information.

The strong link between taste and learning started with human evolution. It was a venue in which humanity learned and formed memories usually linked with either pleasure or pain for survival. A bitter or sour taste generally was an indication of poisonous, inedible, or rotting food; sweet and salty food in contrast is often a sign of food that is rich in nutrients and safer to eat. The strong link continues with other memories that can be triggered that are related to taste, which can also evoke feelings that can be used for framing new information to form new learning.

Taste is an important component of LEP learning because it can influence memory and trigger experiences that relate to concepts being learned through the many taste dimensions. The job of taste as a sense was extremely important to the survival of the human species, and existing taste memories were always retrieved to be compared with new information. New food that was consumed formed new information, feelings, and new knowledge that extended from the existing knowledge. For example, "it tastes like chicken" was a taste comparison to existing memories, which now included new information of the other food that was not, but tasted like, chicken. This expanded comparison is how LEP operates when it expands the understanding of the concept and reinforces the prior LEP memory, which makes it easier to recall later. The trick is to trigger the right memory to expand the concept's definition correctly and in a way that can be retrieved through a representative memory hack later.

Taste has been studied extensively. Typically, there are five tastes identified: salty, bitter, sweet, sour, and umami. However, research by Keast and Costanzo (2015) indicates that oleogustus (fat) as a taste should be added to the mix. Fat offers students another direction to follow to connect to new information. Regardless of which taste is used, or how the memory of taste was evoked, whether through actually taste or feelings of something having to do with taste when connecting concepts being learned, any memory of taste or feeling linked with it, that is appropriate for the true definition of the concept, will be a good fit to expand the concept's understanding and applications.

Remind students that taste elicits a narrative, which is why it is an excellent tool for LEP learning and long-term memory retention. Taste can be associated with things all humanity shares when they navigate through life, such as personal struggles, happy times, any important life events, divorces, weddings, and so on. Taste can bring memories of intense negative or positive emotions or memories of romantic feelings. The taste of food or just thinking about tasting food can trigger memories, not just about the food but the whole experience, the place, setting, who was present, atmosphere, and so on. Just thinking about comfort food can immediately bring back a memory of a specific time or place, or any internal state of the mind and body. All these memories are resources of existing knowledge that can be triggered and brought back to be used as points of reference to expand concept understanding and new learning.

Taste has a long evolutionary history and is perfectly poised to be a bottomless well of memories that can assist and inform current and future learning. Humanity is continuously evaluating, assessing, and comparing information through taste and forming expanded memories and understanding of new information. LEP learning is proactive and with full awareness uses the experiences of taste as one of the primary methods in which to frame new information for understanding new information and to remember it in the long-term.

Hear

Hearing or aural perception is the ability to perceive sound. Sound can quickly trigger memories of experiences that may be connected to new information being learned and vastly assist with new learning. As with all the sensory senses, the sensory cortex of the brain receives and interprets data from the ears. Vibrations cause sound waves. Research shows that most people have poor memory for sound, although some can very effectively learn by sound and even prefer that style of learning.

Memories of sound although not usually the strongest in the memory senses for recollection can and should also be used to form new learning. Sound repetition allows people to memorize concepts in a quick but usually short-term way, as when students repeat information to cram for tests. Sounds can also create very intense long-lasting memories depending on the situation and can be very effective when searching memories for moments that new information must be connected to in order to create a framework of new understanding.

Sound is particularly effective in triggering flashbacks, both positive and negative. The flashbacks can be of a traumatic event, perhaps the sound of an ambulance or a firetruck, or of pleasant events such as the sound of waves that bring back wonderful memories of a summer vacation. Thus, sound memories, unique to each student's experience, can be used as a trigger to remember information that can be used to frame the new concept and expand its understanding.

Auditory learners' memories can be tapped using any sound music, poems, stage, lectures, and any other auditory stimuli. The brain processes auditory information differently than the other senses; thus, students who are inclined to prefer listening as a preference for learning or who have strong listening skills are ideal participants to utilize the sound memories to learn and remember new information. One of the best ways to utilize the hearing sense in the classroom and allow space where memory triggers as related to material being learned can sprout is to include small group discussion segments immediately after the lecture.

In a group setting where students can express themselves using sound (spoken words) generated through the discussion format, they are offered the opportunity to compare their current understanding of the topic they learned in the lesson of the day and share memories of their past experiences of how the concepts relates to other people's perception of sounds, with each other. Thus, they create numerous and varied opportunities for triggering many memories in and through each other's concept understanding, viewpoint, and stories. Sharing information through sound from various lens perspective vastly assists in concept comprehension and memory retention, in all students, but particularly for students who prefer to learn through sound.

Touch

Touch and bodily kinesthetic sensory learning is slated for students who learn by touch, or physical body experiences. Any memories having to do with the physical body, activities, movement, or sense of touch is usually aligned with the bodily kinesthetic student preferences when framing new information. Body factors; sports; an exercise or other physical activity memories, pleasurable such as gardening, running, or walking; or even memories of hand gestures or other body language movements to communicate like dancing, touch, kiss, sex, that focus on touch are suited for new learning to the student with a focus on the physical experience. Negative experiences such as being hit, or seeing other hit can also elicit touch memories and can be used for learning. Bodily kinesthetic students, as haptic students, rely on touch to learn. These students love to learn by doing, are very hands-on in their learning approach and like having direct involvement. Thus offering bodily examples and how to use their bodily-kinesthetic preferences when teaching them new information would assist them to trigger memories to relate to the concept under study and would assist them in learning how to trigger the process within themselves when needed.

The touch sense is a powerful memory trigger and has a wide range of use that can be used to frame new information for understanding and memory retention. Something as simple as a feel of satin can bring back a wide range of memories and expand on the incoming information. The role of touch is very important in learning and memory because it is the interface between our physical bodies and the outside world that makes it a prime instrument for students in connecting to new information. It will be up to the student to choose the correct touch memory as appropriate to the concept under study to frame new information for expanded understanding and applications.

Touch can trigger memories because it can inform and clarify learning as it is a fundamental part of our daily lives and our experience. The sensation of touch is used to gather information about our surroundings and as a way to establish trust and social bonds with others. In his book, *Touch: The Science of the Hand, Heart, and Mind*, Linden suggests that the "genes, cells and neural circuits involved in the sense of touch have been crucial to creating our unique human experience." Linder suggests that a human touch powerfully influences lives and can affect everything from consumer choice to how people love and heal. He emphasized the significance of interpersonal touch as related to social bonding and individual development, and the importance of the sensory and emotional context to work together to create new experiences. LEP learning takes into consideration both the sensory output of physical touch and the emotional context to trigger memories that will create new and expanded understanding of the concepts under study.

The sense of touch can be a valuable trigger, a tool for new learning on many levels. Touch is controlled by a network of nerve endings, which give our brains a wealth of information about the environment. All memories of touch—interactive touch, such as kissing or shaking hands (Goold & Hummell, 1993), and noninteractive touch, such as rubbing, scratching, and so on—can elicit memories that can be expanded to accommodate future learning and better memory retention.

The process of how touch is processed in the brain is limited relative to what is known about the other sensory systems. Neuroscience research indicates that there are two pathways in the brain for processing touch information. The first is sensory, which includes facts like texture, pressure, and so on, and the second process includes social and emotional information. Linden (2015) describes the touch sense as an important interface between the sense of touch and emotional responses that affect human social interactions, general health, and development. In operation the combination of both sensory and emotional can produce different results. For example, the same touch can feel differently upon the encounter. Touching a partner's hand during a romantic time will feel different when touching your partners hand during an adversarial event, even though it is the same hands, in the same environmental setting, such as their home, but both can be used as an experience that can form new learning.

Touch experiences are very formidable and hold fast in memory. Touch triggers are also very effective in retrieval of prior memories. LEP memory triggers search the deep well of touch memories and encourage educators to continue to instruct their students to critically think using the touch experiences for new learning. An example of how to use touch memory triggers should be illustrated in a class by the educator or at least demonstrated as to how to trigger memories relative to the content the educator is presenting through the touch sense.

Practicing with sensory memory triggers should become routine in an LEP classroom. Students should use their sensory experiences from their five senses either independently or in combination to use as memory triggers to connect to new information whenever possible to assist in the new learning. Students should practice with the touch and all sensory memory triggers and use the LEP worksheet Activity 6 to record information. This is an engaging activity that allows students to work with the material they are learning and expand the concept understanding in various ways. (See figure 4.2.)

Figure 4.2 LEP Sensory Memory Triggers Worksheet

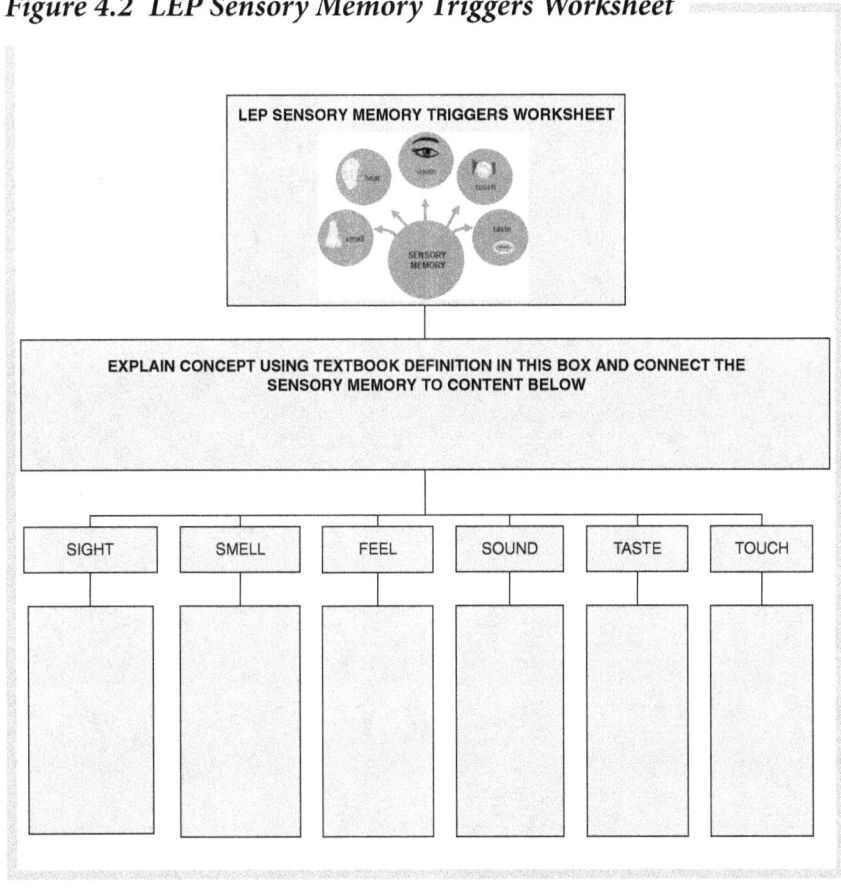

CHAPTER FIVE

LEP ATTRIBUTES MEMORY TRIGGER CATEGORIES

Categorizing LEP Memory Triggers by Innate Attributes
Linguistic/Word Attribute
Logical Attribute
Musical Attribute
Interpersonal Attribute
Intrapersonal Attribute
Naturalistic Attribute
Existential Attribute
Spiritual Attribute
Conditioned Response
LEP Learning Attribute Triggers in Combination

CATEGORIZING LEP MEMORY TRIGGERS BY INNATE ATTRIBUTES

An ability is a skill. An attribute is much more personal, as it is a quality, a natural characteristic of something or someone. LEP's teaching and learning methods draw from students' innate attributes and integrate them and their strengths to process and form new learning in a uniquely personal way. In many ways, LEP's learning attribute triggers are aligned with and were based on the definitions of some of Howard Gardner's (1993) theory of intelligences, which include linguistic, logical, musical, interpersonal, intrapersonal, naturalist, and existentialism. However, and although they may be viewed as similar in some respects, LEP attributes do not operate in quite the same way as Gardner's (1993) theory of intelligences although they are based in the some of the same core ideology.

Gardner (1993) concluded that students learn in ways that are identifiably unique. LEP teaching methods agree. Gardner's (1993) multiple intelligence theory emerged from psychology to demonstrate that human beings have multiple intelligences that are unique to them that they use for learning. LEP teaching methods also concur that students learn uniquely from their own innate learning blueprints and that these blueprints can hold valuable and effective learning strategies unique to each student's learning needs. To tap into those blueprints, LEP learning uses the existing information stored in each student's brain that can be triggered to frame new information through the lens of the students' strongest attribute, thereby assisting them to learn in a method that is aligned with their most effective learning approach and offers them the opportunity to expand on the concept(s) definition(s) through their strongest attribute.

In addition to linguistic, logical, musical, interpersonal, intrapersonal, naturalist, and existentialism, LEP includes the spiritual attribute and the conditioned response. The spiritual attribute is the immortal entity of the person, rooted in a belief system of a Universal Consciousness, higher power, God, or Spirit, whatever the appropriate term unique to each person may be that guides them from this inward counsel. This added step connects Western education with Easter philosophy and offers students an option for the holistic approach in personal learning. God is firmly planted in many students' mind, and many people make their decisions, adjust their behavior, and perceive the world through a higher perspective of God. Not to include God would be to limit some students' experiences and would be a great disservice to students who learn through a personal connection to that higher source or consciousness.

The conditioned response offers another path of innate exploration for new learning and is included among the LEP learning attributes. So much of the human existence and behaviors stem from the conditioned reactions and responses; thus, it would not be possible to discuss the lived experience phenomenon in learning without including conditioning. Conditioned responses are also integral in learning, and are included in the LEP trigger attribute paradigm, as things like habits, repetitious behavior, routines, patterns, and so on manifest automatically, and these experiences can be very creative instruments for connecting new to existing knowledge to form new learning.

Linguistic/Word Attribute

Traditionally, linguistic students are wordsmiths by nature and show their greatest strengths in using words for expression. Since linguistic students express themselves well, these students should find reflecting on memories that tie into concepts and describing the connection between them with relative ease. These students should be encouraged to offer examples in descriptions of how the concept relates to their existing knowledge and how they can expand upon their definitions and applications.

All students have linguistic (verbal) attribute and sensitivity to the sounds, meanings, and rhythms of words, but linguistic students prefer using words, both in speech and in writing, more than students with strengths in other learning attributes. They love vocabulary, and love to read and write. Word games, reading, even sound of words, like lyrics and songs, are a draw for linguistic students. Since verbal style encompasses both written and spoken word, educators should direct students with strengths in the linguistic attributes to focus on memories that relate to the concept(s) through experiences with the written or spoken word. Students should be encouraged to describe in writing the memories of their lived experiences relative to the material being learned and include written descriptions of how the concept that they are learning about operates in their life to help them frame the information for better understanding, and quicker recollection when needed.

Phrases that can trigger memories, word games, and rhymes (if appropriate to the subject matter) can also serve as memory triggers to recall information that may expand the understanding of new information in linguistically strong students. Even stories that the students have read or wrote about can trigger memories to explain and expand on the new concept(s) they are learning. Educators should encourage students to play with the meaning or sound of words when searching memories for the right connection to frame the new concept, and be creative in their approach, however always being careful that the concept definition is authentic to the academic interpretation.

Logical Attribute

Logical students prefer using logic, reasoning, and the analytical systems of their mind. In many math and science-oriented courses, this thinking approach can offer a limitless well of wisdom students can tap into to explain new concepts they are learning. Logical attributes, which include mathematical and analytical nature, allow students to think conceptually, analytically, and abstractly. These students have the capacity to discern logical and numerical patterns, and thus should be encouraged to recognize patterns between concepts they are learning and linking that information to the existing knowledge or concepts under study.

The brain taps prior experiences or automatic associations to reframe the existing information to form new knowledge in a methodological way. Students strong in the logical attribute category should be encouraged to access LEP memories that had to do with experiences based in logical, analytical, or mathematical reasoning, whenever possible to learn new information. Logical mathematical students can connect to existing memories of numbers, formulas, and calculations and review problems and issues in a systematic way to see where and how they can connect new information to concepts already learned.

Numerical targets, to-do lists, logical reasoning experiences, and remembering through brain teasers are ideally suited for the LEP logical learner to trigger the existing knowledge in order to expand it to form new information. Additionally, using numbers or the logical analytical approach as memory triggers to access the existing information in the human mind sets up the structure to frame the new memory in a lucid, analytical manner as it draws upon prior experiences, which may shed light on the new concept. In this way the existing information is understood from the strength of the students' logical attribute and integrated with the concepts under study to expand and form new knowledge and concept applications.

Musical Attribute

The effect of music on all students, but in particular musically inclined students, cannot be understated. Music engages students' minds and the senses; it can take them on imaginary journeys, help them relax, calm them down enough to focus, and help them remember information. If you have taught long enough, you will notice that musical songs and rhymes stay with students; it is the cues of melody and beat that help them remember the words in a very engaging way. Thus, music or memories of music or words or the experiences or feeling associated with music can be used to explain concepts under study or to remember information being learned long term.

The musical learner usually likes and can learn through music and associations with song and remembering concepts (Davis, 2007). Thus, since musical learners prefer to use music and sound to learn and remember information, this choice should be made available to them as a way to retrieve information from their memories to associate and expand on current learning. Musical students can easily connect new concepts to existing memories having to do with the concept through music. Additionally, activities with music can create the neural connections necessary for various abilities such as math and literacy, making learning engaging and less challenging.

Generally, musical students benefit greatly by using their musical attribute strength in the learning and memory process. Educators should explain the concept of musical attributes (where appropriate and applicable) to students to make them aware of this attribute that may assist them to learn and remember new information. Various experiences with music, learning music, instruments, and so on are all experiences that can be tapped into to expand the existing knowledge, depending on the concepts being learned. LEP musical memory triggers should be encouraged by the educators since music can evoke not only strong memories but also emotions, which can also be used to explain and expand concept definitions and applications, particularly in well-suited disciplines like the arts and social sciences.

Interpersonal Attribute

It has been said that "you first need to live the experience and only then you can learn the lesson." But learning the lesson is not enough; with LEP you must use the memory of the lesson to learn new information in a continuous cycle building upon its interpretation to integrate the existing information with new knowledge to form new wisdom. Interpersonal attributes are an infinite pool of experiences that can be used to expand prior learning and replace it with new learning. Students who show interpersonal strengths of being are aware of personal thoughts and how their actions and feelings affect others usually have very strong interpersonal attributes. As such, they have at their disposal a boundless database of information within them to link with new information to form new knowledge.

Interpersonal communication teaches many lessons and offers experiences through a myriad of life exchanges. All types of interpersonal memories should and can be used to connect to concepts being learned to expand their definitions. Lessons learned in life personally through interpersonal exchanges can be associated with all kinds of new concepts being learned, which can help explain or give students a fresh perspective on the concept(s) and how they can operate in real life. All communication between human beings is interpersonal, and interactions such as people asking for advice, experiences that may have been enjoyed, experiences of sharing ideas through conversation or working through problems in a group, or any social activity that includes other people like card games or board games are all memories that can be and should be used as a resource for current and future learning.

Students with strong interpersonal attributes are very social and prefer to work with others. They have the capacity to detect and respond appropriately to the moods, motivations, and desires of others and usually have the desire to learn whether and how life can be connected to what they are learning now. The social science and humanities disciplines are ideally suited for concept interpretations through the memories of lived experiences of students who are strong in interpersonal attributes as they deal with human behavioral factors. Thus, students in these types of courses or students who possess strong interpersonal attributes should be encouraged to work within the interpersonal attribute sphere, and look at social occasions, relationships, and communication to trigger memories to connect the new information to expand its interpretation(s) and application(s).

Intrapersonal Attribute

The educator should put an effort in assisting intrapersonal students engage in the LEP sharing of information concept. Traditionally, intrapersonal students are very skilled in reflective thoughts; thus, since LEP operates within the "inquisitive reflection" sphere, these students are prime to utilize LEP learning to look into their minds to retrieve information that they need to connect to current learning. Students who are strong in interpersonal attributes know themselves and their motivations, and appreciate the value of their feelings as learning tools, but they generally do not like to share themselves or information in public settings.

Since LEP functions within the sphere of sharing information not only with the educator but also with class, at first, some students may not feel comfortable in disclosing personal information. Intrapersonal students can be very private, introspective, and unwilling to share information. If they choose not to share in class, this should be respected as they can still participate in the process and make their connections to the material being learned in their personal way without sharing the information with their classmates.

But it has been the experience of LEP educators that, generally, in a short time students understand that the information they are sharing is not private, but from a personal perspective, and feel more comfortable with the LEP learning structure. Even intrapersonal students who normally do not easily share information do so with LEP because they see the benefits of sharing information as it relates to the concepts learned with their classmates. Most students quickly adjust and follow the other students' lead and ease of matter in the way they disclose information and fully participate in the process, reaping their own rewards and enjoying the process of sharing information with others in a classroom setting often for the first time in their life.

Students strong in intrapersonal attributes see the world from a deep personal insight perspective. They live in a world of self-knowledge and understanding and know their weaknesses and strengths. Intrapersonal students can explore memories of self-analysis or reflecting on past events and personal hobbies. They can explore reflections of self-development or any other thoughts or tasks they can to appropriately connect the subject matter to and expand its definitions.

Students should be guided by educators to use their intrapersonal attribute strengths to connect new concepts to existing knowledge through a more mental, independent, or rather individual thought state. Memories of such experiences or events are usually not private, but it is useful knowledge that can be used, when appropriate, to expand some concept(s) under study. Intrapersonal students have the capacity to be self-aware and in tune with feelings, values, hidden beliefs, and thinking processes. Intrapersonal students like to work alone and prefer self-study over working with others; they are aware of themselves and how they affect the world around them. These experiences offer students information to better explain the concepts being learned.

Naturalist Attribute

Naturalistic students are naturally aware of their surrounds and environments, which is logical since according to Howard Gardner (1993), the naturalistic student is sensitive to nature. Naturalist attribute is the students' ability to recognize and sense patterns and make connection to elements of nature (Gardner, 1993). Naturalistic students learn best through LEP when learning through natural phenomena experiences usually through outdoor experiences and connected in some way to nature, occurrence in nature, or using memories of these happenings.

Naturalist students have an excellent natural orientation, or the ability to identify with living organisms and their environments. They usually have a strong affinity to the outside world, animals, plants, and/or pets. They hold an affinity for a wide range of things from nature, fossils, butterflies, feathers, shell fish, flowers, fields, clouds, sunsets, rainbows, moon, and so on, and have the associated knowledge within them at their disposal to use for current and future learning.

Naturalistic students have a real interest in the welfare of the world. Observations in naturalistic students is strong, and educators should encourage them to use their affinity for nature as triggers to recall information that can help with expanding the concepts under study's and their application(s). Educators should encourage students strong in the naturalistic attribute, or students who are interested in the sciences as a discipline, to use this innate tool to draw information from their minds to frame new information for the comprehension of current and the expansion of future learning.

Existential Attribute

LEP existential students question life, more specifically the meaning of life. Existentialism is a philosophical perception that centers on the experience an individual has and the way they interpret that experience. Existential attribute strong students have a heightened sensitivity and capacity to tackle the deep questions about human existence, in a uniquely diverse and highly independent way relative to the human existence and their environment. Additionally, these students do not prescribe to a God or a source per se for guidance but instead choose to perceive their experiences and meaning attributed to them as defined from the outside of spiritual forces or influences.

Existential attributes tackle profound questions such as, What is consciousness? Or what is the meaning of life? Gardner (1993) summed up existential intelligence (which LEP existential attribute is based on) as "individuals who exhibit the proclivity to pose and ponder questions about life, death, and ultimate realities." This explanation is wide ranging, and answers will be highly subjective. But it is an area that everyone can relate to or has some opinion about. And for the existential students who do not believe in a God or a source that directs life, it is also an important area that has great depth in terms of experiences that may be explored, bringing to surface information that can be used to explain current learning and expanded to form new applications of the concepts under study.

Existentialism is just a philosophical position, but many students use it as a way of life, or as a perceptual lens with which they see the world and get the answers they seek. Their observations form the experiences and memories that LEP learning uses to connect to and expand the information of concepts. Existential beliefs are rooted in the acceptance that life is understandable relative to the person's perception, and each person's experience of life is different and holds different meanings for different people.

Existential students contribute vastly to class or group discussions when working with new information because of their uncanny ability and direct approach to be real about facts and to take the responsibility for their life decisions. Generally, instead of focusing on religious beliefs for support systems, these students describe focusing on finding solutions to their problems without the assistance of an omnipotent force, which usually sprouts a lively discussion that often can be appropriately connected to the information being learned. It is important to note that when working with existentialism in a purer sense within the LEP spectrum, existentialism does not deny the aspects of biology, psychology, and other sciences; it simply claims that people cannot be fully understood in those terms. Thus, students deeply rooted in existentialism will most likely possess a gold mind of distinctive information and experiences that can be shared with other students to explain concept(s) and offer various concept applications for further understanding and clarification of the new information.

Spiritual Attribute

LEP teaching methods include the spiritual attribute in its learning methods after significant student feedback indicated that students not only were firmly rooted in their spiritual beliefs and believed they had a soul, but believed their values, moral, ethical and life principles were drawn from the spiritual principle. Spiritual attribute students possess the awareness that they live in a collaborative existence with God, or a Universal Higher Consciousness, who is their support system, and never-ending life source. LEP teaching and learning can use these spiritually based experiences, and any others within the spiritual attribute sphere for explaining and expanding current concepts, their applications, and future learning.

The definition of spirituality is very ambiguous and fluid as it is personally subjective to interpretation of the beholder and what it means to them. LEP teaching methods use a general interpretation of spirituality as a quality common to all people. For example, even though students may worship at different places and have various religious beliefs, they can still share in the energy of 'spirituality,' a general belief in a God, Universal Higher Consciousness or any other deity that guides their life. The focus of the spiritual attribute is placed on the internal voice, not guided through any rituals, practices or traditions from external sources.

Spiritual attributes which include the soul energy deals with a holistic approach to learning. Since there is a general belief system in spirituality that a soul is created by God, in the student with strong spiritual attributes, God takes center stage from which everything emanates. Without getting caught up in the exact definition of spirituality, or a soul, for that definition is most likely different for everyone, spirituality for the purposes of this book is understood as concerned with the human spirit and the soul attribute allows for a greater opportunity to have access to an invisible spiritual reality that connects the person, and concepts learned, in deeper ways to include an omnipresence of God, or a Universal Higher Consciousness that governs human kind from spiritual realms.

Spirituality is an internal practice, not external such as formalized religion. Though all religions emphasize spirituality, a person does not have to be religious to be spiritual, and often is not, nor do they partake in any organized religion. The spiritual attribute includes the ability to view beauty, life, experience, and truth from a divine perspective of being supported by the Universe, God, the Source and so on relative to the students' life experiences, memories, and perceptions. The insights gained from the human spirit lens can infinitely assist students to expand on concepts they are learning and should be utilized whenever appropriate.

Most students that operate from the spiritual attributes perspective believe that a human being is both corporeal and spiritual, and always immortal. These students quiet themselves and practice listening to their inner being, their higher power, using prayer and communication with God, or personal deity for guidance and direction. This internal work and life's choices as made from the students' spiritual perspective provides them with an unlimited pool of memories of helpful scenarios that can be rediscovered and applied to new concepts to increase their understanding. And if shared appropriately with the class, and when applicable, always ensuring all discussion is relative to concepts under study, can vastly expand concept/s definitions from a uniquely personal vantage point. Very often through this distinctive spiritual lens students can offer rich and unique applications of how to apply the concepts they are learning about in a daily life of a person.

The spiritual attribute is seen as foundation for values and ideals in a student who lives their life from the spiritual perspective. Their belief in a higher spiritual or universal power is such a major part of their life that it is hard for them not to connect God or some form of a Universal Higher Consciousness that oversees humanity to their learning. LEP takes advantage of this existing personal connection to personal deities when it asks students to see concepts from a spiritual lens when learning new information (if applicable) for concept understanding. The spiritual context is inner experience but is just as powerful to use to increase understanding and create personal memory triggers to retrieve any information that can explain current information as any of the other innate attributes, and should be encouraged as a tool for learning new information whenever possible.

CONDITIONED RESPONSE

Similarly, as with priming, learning through experiences and memories of conditioned responses is naturally aligned with the LEP teaching and learning methods. Conditioning is a psychological principle where an organism learns new behavior via the process of association, usually through repetition (Pavlov, 1897). It is a type of learning in which the stimulant acquires the capacity to cause a response that can be predicted because of repetitive associations. For example, in some settings, the words "say cheese" might be followed by a camera flash and a smile on the part of the photographed person. The words "say cheese" (unconditioned stimuli) are associated with the camera (neutral stimuli) and produce a smile (conditioned stimuli). A sneeze can produce, the common expression of 'God bless you,' followed by the predictable 'thank you.'

There are various ways LEP educators can use the attributes of conditioning in the classroom setting to enhance learning and encourage their students to be aware of their own programed conditioning and use that information as a tool for new learning. This can be a fun activity for students, an opportunity to learn about themselves and their conditioned responses of which they may not be aware of, and simultaneously learn about the concept at hand and how it can apply to them and their life. By asking students simple questions and planting thoughts in their heads, such as, "Think about your past lived experiences, what conditioned responses do you have? How do they play into the concept being learned? How do you think they can relate?," educators should have examples of how the concept can be connected to conditioned responses using their own personal examples to assist students to make their own personal connections.

Once students discover their own conditioning outputs that are applicable and appropriate for the concept(s) they are learning, they can use this information to connect to present and future learning in a very unique and personal way. Using their critical thinking skills and exploring their memories through linking the topic through association to their conditioned lived experiences can be personally rewarding and very effective in learning and the memory retention of the learned material.

LEP includes conditioning in the learning paradigm because conditioning often influences how, why, and where students draw meaning from. Students have a lifetime of conditioned responses that they possess and can draw from. Everything engrained from childhood, culture, gender, economic status, biases, prejudices, suppositions, and so on is material ready to be used at the will of the student to connect to new information to expand the concept definitions in a personal way. These conditioned responses are very important in the students' lives because they are tied to perceptions, and this is habitually how students see their world very often without even realizing that they are viewing it and themselves through this conditioned bias.

Learning new information through the lens of conditioning can be a powerful way to create meaning and remember the information long term. Connecting conditioning to lived experiences always ensuring that if fits the content under study often assists students in better understanding their own personal conditioning functions and how this available knowledge about themselves can help their future learning. Making association between concepts students are learning and themselves increases the significance of the material being learned in a personal way and assists in easier retrieval of this information when needed.

USING LEP MEMORY TRIGGER ATTRIBUTES IN COMBINATION

All LEP learning trigger attributes are of equal value. All learning draws upon the innate attributes of students regardless of what they are and helps them to work smarter and not harder. LEP's only real interest lies in how it can help students and educators trigger the existing information within students regardless of which attribute they connect with the strongest, and letting that attribute/s serve as a tool for framing new information for concept expansion and future learning in an engaging way so that students not only learn in a personal way but also enjoy the learning process, which greatly helps in class retention.

LEP assists in that process because of the personal connection of the material being learned to the students' personal attributes, offering them an awareness of how they see the world, and the opportunity to use this same attributional lens to learn new information. In this way, LEP teaching methods promote active learning through students' innate learning attributes as a trigger tool to expand their existing knowledge base as applied to the new material learned and increases personal engagement in the content.

The student looks for "meaning" and uses existing associations between the new information received and the existing information already stored in their long-term memory through their strongest attribute, or a combination of attributes, to form an expanded meaning, creating new knowledge. In the LEP learning process more is more. Using memory triggers in combination with each other greatly expands concept interpretations and offers several lenses in which to view the concept application/s. Using past experience to define current concepts through the lens of the students' innate learning attributes gives the concepts both academic and personal meaning, which will move the information from short-term to long-term memory quicker because of the personal or real-world application. Ultimately, the advantage is that students remain engaged in the learning process because they find the concepts meaningful to their lives, which helps them to be generally more focused, attentive, and more willing to participate, which in turn helps everyone enjoy the course and achieve higher learning outcomes.

Students may possess multiple variations in the strength of their innate learning attributes when triggering existing memories to connect to new information. They can use one or as recommended combination of attributes they feel are their strongest. Depending on how the information is presented, their preference, and the strength(s) of the learning attributes that was engaged, each student will vary in what trigger attribute was used, how many trigger attributes were used, how well they understood the information, and how much information can be retained.

Processing information for understanding and memory retention while utilizing their learning attributes as personal triggers gives students an opportunity to master new information and increase memory retention in an innately personal way. Additionally, aligning students with their innate learning attributes to trigger and learn new information will result in a personal intellectual undertaking that offers students the opportunity to learn and remember by using themselves and their triggered memories as application tools for new knowledge and enjoy the process as they learn. To help students understand how to work with their personal attributes for learning, educators should include some time allotted for students to practice with the LEP Trigger Attribute Recording Worksheets (see Activities 7, 8, 9)

Figure 5.1 LEP Trigger Attribute Recording Worksheet

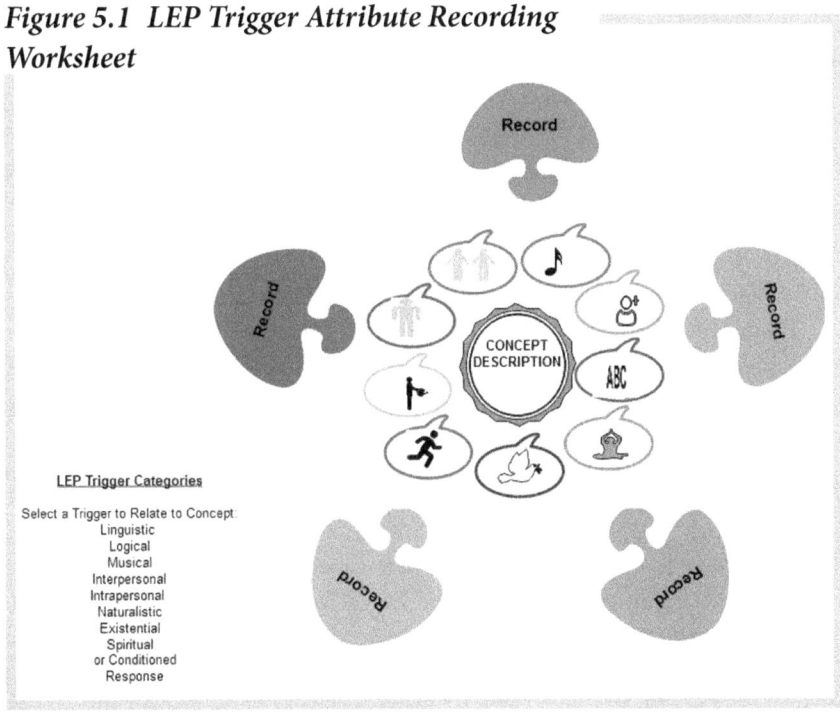

during class time. For optimal results, opportunities should be offered to students in a structured atmosphere of sharing where students can work in groups, with the same concepts and share their information, clarify, ask questions, and discuss the worksheet within their group and the educator as they work through each section.

One of the simplest ways to introduce students to the LEP trigger attributes learning is to have them work with the LEP trigger attribute activity (see figure 5.1). Using trigger activities is "reflective"; thus, students should take time and inquisitively reflect on each of the sections before working with or recording information.

- At the center of the diagram the students record the concept, with a true definition, as imparted by the educator, textbooks, and so on. The concept definition should be clear, short, and precise using key words to summarize the concept.

- The next section consists of attribute images as representations of each category. Using inquisitive reflection, the students should review each image to see which symbols resonate with them the most relative to the subject matter at hand. Again, time should be spent in looking at the images in the sections and allowing the images to trigger memories that relate to the concept. (People in general have a remarkable ability to remember images; thus, images are usually the most efficient tools to trigger memories.)

- The following section offers a glimpse of some of the natural attributes of that particular image in brief text descriptions. This category clarifies the learning trigger in that particular section that can be used to process their thoughts. It organizes their thinking based on the suggestive words and identifies path tracks to trigger information as it relates to the concepts within that LEP trigger category.

- The next section offers expanded definitions of the attributes for each category students should use to trigger their memories. Keeping the expanded definitions in mind, the student reviews the LEP learning attributes and selects the category that best resonates with the concept. Again, the student should be moving through the activity in a slow pace inquisitively reflecting on each section, searching the mind for the right memory that can frame the new information and expand the concept definition and its application.

- The next section offers a space to record the memory trigger associated with the concept being learned. Once memory is triggered and the concept is linked with existing memories that will expand the concept definition and its application, the student must record the information. Recording information in writing will complete trigger reinforcement and assist in the retention of information in long-term memory.

- In the last section the students should visually doodle or sketch an image of the memory trigger they used to retrieve this memory as it relates to the concepts learned. Sketching the trigger links it to the concept and immensely assists in memory recall when the information is needed later.

CHAPTER SIX

LEP CONTEXT MEMORY TRIGGERS

PHYSICAL CONTEXT TRIGGERS
EMOTIONAL CONTEXT TRIGGERS
MENTAL CONTEXT TRIGGERS
ENVIRONMENTAL CONTEXT TRIGGERS
PERSONAL BELIEF CONTEXT TRIGGERS
MORAL CONTEXT (CONSCIENCE) TRIGGERS

LEP TRIGGER CONTEXT TREE

Choose your Category to Connect to Concept

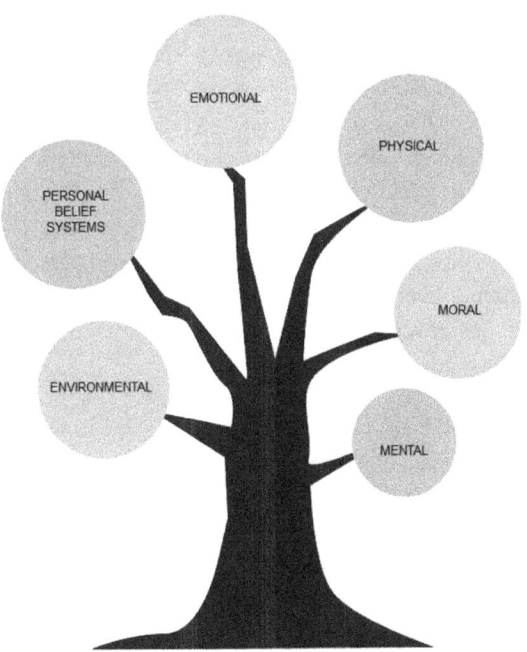

CATEGORIZING LEP MEMORY TRIGGERS BY CONTEXTS

One of the most important aspects of working with LEP contextual memory triggers is that it offers students an instant meaning of the structure of the concept they are learning and a glimpse into how it could be personally applied. Unlike LEP attributes, which focus on students' innate learning abilities the LEP tree categorizes memory triggers through various lived experience contextual elements that focus not only on the definitions but also on the structure of concepts from a personal lived experience knowledge and perspective.

Categorizing triggers through personal life meaning structures offers students the added step of structural information to be presented through contextual meanings. The contextual meaning gained from the categories of emotional, physical, mental, environmental, moral, and personal belief systems contexts assists students in forming a structure that conveys concept meaning of new information in a uniquely personal way. Contextual triggers also offer students an opportunity for framing the concepts using academic definitions and can demonstrate how the knowledge of the concepts under study fits independently and collectively in the students' life, or the world at large.

All living is learning. Learning is the acquisition of knowledge through experience and is a key process in human behavior. This is a key reason LEP teaching methods place the lived experience at center stage when learning new information. Research indicates that life is a significant qualifying experience, but the learning from that experience is unique because it differs from one person to another. The meaning gained from the experience is unique to each person, even though they might have shared the same experience because their perception of it and what happened is perceived through their own contextual lens. This is one of the reasons why it is imperative that students use their personal experiences when learning new concepts for understanding. As new knowledge viewed from personal vantage points based on the students' lived experiences increases comprehension in a faster and more rooted way. Moreover, knowledge associated with personal connections can be retrieved with less effort when needed later.

Merriam and Clark (2006) explain the underlying structure of the significance of life-experience learning and how a particular life experience can become a significant learning experience for one person, but not another. This occurs as a result of the uniqueness of people and how the world is perceived and interpreted. Merriam and Clark (2006) contend that for learning to be significant, it must affect the learner personally either by resulting in an expansion of skills, sense of self, or life perspective or by precipitating a transformation, and must be subjectively valued by the learner. Thus, material, if taught properly, must be made personally meaningful to students or they must perceive it as so.

Meaning making within the LEP contextual categories makes concepts relevant to students and allows them to understand their life experience and how this experience can help them learn and remember new information. The LEP teaching method is successful because it is based upon personal perception and students' own subjectivity and/or imagination to make meaningful connections to what they are learning and know why this is important to them, which is invaluable in the concept application process. The end result is positive, as even when the material becomes challenging or confusing, students continue to be motivated to persist and use their subjectivity to connect the concept to their experiences to spark an understanding of the concept within themselves in a personal way by using one of the contextual categories to trigger information.

The same subjectivity that determines which experience holds the most importance to the person grows wisdom and can significantly increase long-term retention of new learning. Results from wisdom studies suggest that this is true, since learning from important and meaningful life experiences can foster wisdom (Yang, 2014). Thus, wisdom comes in the form of contextual memories, which can be triggered by each student to tap into to frame new information and retain that information in the long term with greater ease because of the personal connection that was associated with the information.

Learning often boils down to subjectivity, as what is important to one person may not be to another. If the material is deemed unimportant, the attention and engagement of students decrease. If students find the information important to them somehow, attention and engagement increase. Thus, it is recommended to include LEP teaching methods in student learning to achieve these desired results in every course.

Everyone experiences, and everyone remembers. Some memories are stronger than others, but they come from various contextual categories, where they rest ready to be used again. From these contextual memories, students possess the ability to see and understand life as a whole and use this structural information of concepts for current and future learning. The experiences people encounter during their life journey, both negative and positive, are all learning interactions gained while traveling through life acquiring habits, perceptions, opinions, viewpoints, and sentiments which add to their collective view of life, and their contextual representations of themselves and their world. These contextual experiences also serve as their own personal database that assists them in making decisions, problem solving, interacting with others, and so on, which are all learning experiences within themselves and offer a structure to the experience to provide it meaning. LEP learning takes these existing meanings (memories) and expands upon them building upon existing information to integrate it with new knowledge to form new wisdom.

The LEP tree (see chapter 10) gives a general view of contextual categories of experiences and their meanings which may be triggered to retrieve existing information and link it with new knowledge. It represents the evolution of human experiences, which create memories and information that can be used for future learning of new information through the contextual categories of emotional, physical, mental, environmental, moral and personal belief systems contexts. Students can use one or a combination of contextual categories to trigger the right experience, the best-suited memory to create an association between the memory and the concept under study to expand its definition(s). If a memory does not become available the students are encouraged to use their imagination to form personal applications of the concept based on the academic interpretation.

The LEP tree (see Activity 11) shows human connections gained from all types of lived experiences. Everything that is a memory within the students own personal life existence and nucleus can be used to frame and explain concepts under study and be used as a tool to remember that information when needed at a later time. This includes emotions, motivations, and so on that can be used as triggers to find the best memories to relate to the concept. The more personal or intense the memory association to the material being learned, the more effective the trigger to recall the information later.

PHYSICAL CONTEXT TRIGGERS

The human body keeps physical memories of all of its lived experiences. Physical contexts (see figure 6.1) include the experiences and the contextual meaning behind the physical and biological aspects of those memories that can be triggered to form new learning. Learning through the body, experiences and senses or any physical activity like dance can bring knowledge and self-expression, and produce new levels of self-esteem during the learning process as students connect with information and are able to process that information through the lens of one of their strongest attributes. Other experiences involving the body ranging from health, wellness, illness, memories, pain, pleasure, sleeping, eating, exercise, gardening, sex, aging, growing, genetics, healing, physical death memories, and so on are common experiences to all students and can be drawn upon in learning new material.

Figure 6.1 LEP Physical Contexts

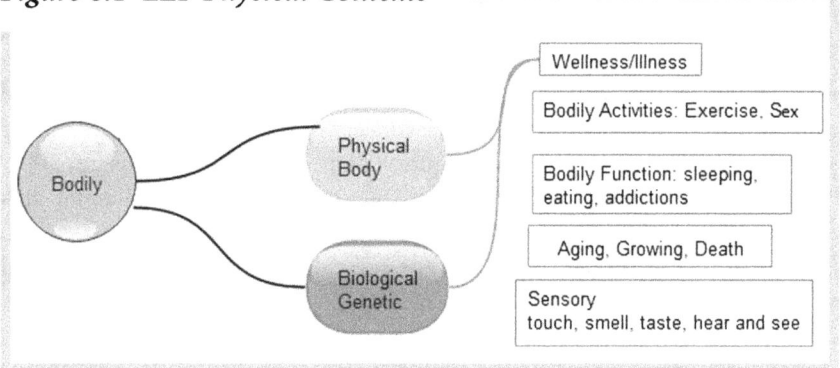

Learning new information through the biological and genetic lens offers students a unique way to approach new information from another context in which they may have existing information or interest. Students can use memories of biological aspects whenever appropriate relative to new concepts being learned and construct new understanding and generalizations that will assist them to apply the information being learned in their life. Using physical aspects as examples in the classroom to explain information is one of the easiest contexts that can be used by educators. For example, everyone can recall being sick, but everyone will remember and associate with the concept "sick" differently based on their memories. Thus the trigger "sick," relative to the concept being learned, is the same as everyone knows the feeling of "sick" but the memory hack of how they understand it and remember it will be different.

Physical memories in general are usually utilized and have been shown to be the most effective in new learning and memory retention of information being learned by students who show bodily kinesthetic tendencies. These students remember most effectively through a hands-on approach instead of textbook or lecture learning formats, but all students should be encouraged to use the physical contextual category whenever appropriate to frame new information for comprehension. The mind within students learns through the experience of sensory information like touch and taste, processes that information, and stores it for future use, but it is in the contextual meaning and emotions behind those occurrences that LEP learning can unearth richer information and use these different venues of understanding as modes for new learning and memory retention of information.

Life's physical experiences are emphasized through the body as an integral part of the learning process because the physical lived experiences and the perceptions made by them are stored in the memory of body. In somatic learning, which refers to "constructing knowledge that engages the body as a site of learning" (Freiler, 2008) the physical model of learning presumes that we are inherently conscious beings, able to learn through our bodily experiences. Thus, since we can learn through the body we can take existing knowledge from our memories as experienced by the body and connect them to new learning to expand concept understanding and applications whenever possible when learning new information. Because of the potency of their strength, as bodily reactions often elicit an intense response as a result of the high spectrum between pleasure and pain, physical sensations can be the perfect fit to recall some memory that can be used for current and future learning. Physical sensations can be very powerful tools in experiencing the world; thus, they are a deep well of stored information that can be linked with new information to form clearer and more personal understanding of new information.

Working with body memories includes felt senses. Felt sense is of the body and can be loosely defined as a "holistic, implicit, bodily sense of a complex situation" or meaning that enables direct access to our bodies through experience" (Gendlin, 1996, p. 56). Felt sense of the body "establishes a link between what we think (our minds) and what we feel (our bodies), or between what we know implicitly (before words come) and what we ultimately write or say (with words) explicitly" (Perl, 2004, p. 5). Thus, this means that the body memories are aware of and have processed both physical and subliminal and felt senses. The physical body carries within it the memories of each human's experiences, but it also carries within it the interpreted senses of the experiences as assigned through meaning by the students.

The physical contextual category should be used as a tool for comprehension whenever and wherever possible. Educators should encourage students to inquisitive reflect using the physical context whenever appropriate to the concepts under study, as their physical context memories may connect new information to existing knowledge giving them an opportunity to easily expand on the concept definition to form new understanding. Learning through experiences of through, and with the body comes natural to students with a strong physical orientation and connections, and those connections can be utilized to form and remember new information.

EMOTIONAL CONTEXT TRIGGERS

What makes memories meaningful is the emotional significance or priority placed on them. Most students view emotions and feelings as interchangeable constituents, but in fact they are different. Emotions can be felt through an emotional experience,

Figure 6.2 LEP Emotional Contexts

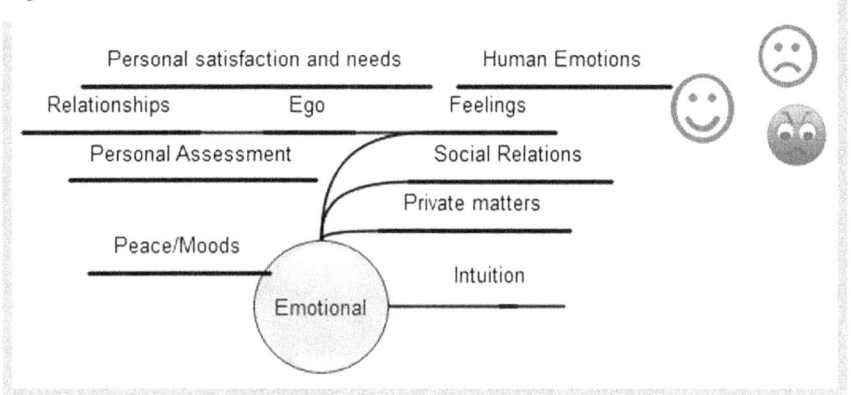

which includes feelings, (see figure 6.2); thus, it is through emotions that people can interpret what those feelings mean. LEP does not get caught up in the intricacies between the two; suffice it to say, both emotions and feelings are very useful tools in the LEP learning comprehension process.

Emotions originate in the brain, more specifically in the limbic system, and arise from memories and reactions to people's lived experiences. Emotions have a significant influence on cognitive processes of a human being such as perception, learning, and memory; thus, emotions are also ideal learning tools to understand new information. Human beings are very emotional beings, and with each extension of emotion, they are constantly creating new memories that can be used to understand new information.

Emotions and meaning that human beings attach to experiences and relationships drive the strength of the ability of recall later. The more significant the emotional tie the stronger the memory and the easier the memory recall. Emotions are an interesting aspect of the human makeup in the way they are formed, and assign meaning to life's energies. Emotions ignite various feelings that students may use to trigger information that is needed for understanding new concepts. Therefore, LEP teaching methods include the emotional context with its unique outputs as a tool to trigger the existing information within the students' brain to form new learning.

As in the physical context, the emotional context is laden with memories that range between pain and pleasure because of their intense nature. Associated with all human emotions a person has ever experienced such as happy, sad, angry, and so on, feelings, intuition, relationships, private matters, or matters of the heart, peace, moods, and many other aspects of emotions that students can use for current and future learning lies the memory of that experience that can be expanded to accommodate new information to frame and form new learning. The emotional context from which a student can pull memories can also include memories of self-control and managing their own emotions in challenging situations. Emotions in many cases are life masters that direct many outputs in our life. Students should use these various emotional outputs to frame new information for understanding.

Educators should encourage all students to work with the emotional context whenever possible to learn new information as the power of feelings is an influential aspect of the human personality and can be used to frame new information for comprehension. Any emotional memory through which inquisitive reflection can connect to the concept under study should be embraced because the power of emotion as exemplified through the memories of feelings is a formidable tool that students can utilize to expand upon existing knowledge and remember new information.

MENTAL CONTEXT TRIGGERS

Experience is just another form of cognition. Students acquire knowledge cognitively through their own personal experience and/or through the experience of others. When students are engaging the mind whether through a backward- (memories) or forward-moving lens using any cognitive processes, they are working within the mental context realm. Working within the broad area of mental contexts through inquisitive reflection, students are opened to a wide range of memories that were formed through mental states of cognitive knowledge.

Cognitive processing includes brain and mind functions that are used by students in all types of thinking skills such as critical, creative, logical, and so on. But all cognitive processes like thoughts and ideas, reflecting, problem solving, suppositions, psychology, and consciousness (see figure 6.3), among others, that can be included to suit or customize a particular course are included in the mental context category within LEP learning. Likewise, perceptions and aspects of personality are included because along with all other cognitive processes, they are capable of combining newly available information and existing memories to produce new mental contexts (states, thoughts, and ideas) and forms of cognitive understanding to assist new learning.

It is important to note that perception is not necessary for cognition. For example, logic in a computer program can be a form of cognition although it is not using the senses of perception. But in LEP learning, cognitive processes of perceptions and personality, which are the characteristics of cognitive patterns within the mental

Figure 6.3 LEP Mental Contexts

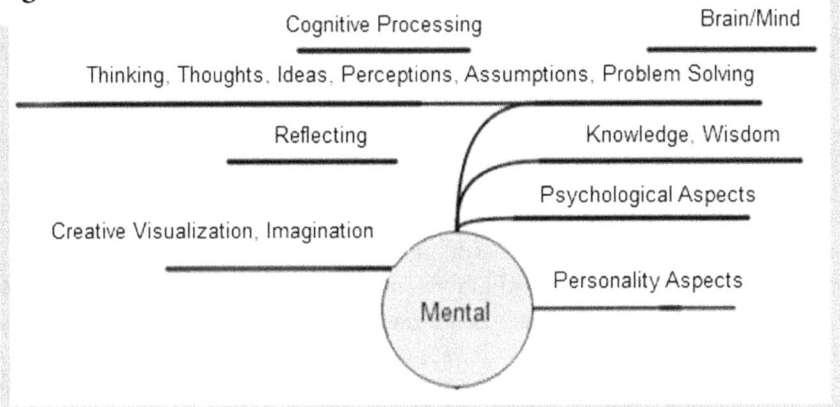

context experiences, are very powerful influences in a person's life and often dictates how information is learned and retained. Perception and personality also affect how people relate to each other in social forums and how they form impressions about themselves and their world. This information once unearthed when needed can be very valuable in current and future learning.

Being aware of how mental contexts operate in the students' life and thinking processes offers another venue to explore when trying to connect concepts being learned to information they already possess. Viewing concepts being learned from a mental context, for example, if a student is thinking of the last time how he or she used critical thinking skills while completing an assignment that required critical thinking skills, can trigger information that can be used for new learning when applying those skills to the current assignment. This connection is usually made quickly because within the familiarity of the existing memories often a framework of what needs to be done materializes. Even if that framework lacks a strong foundation, it is usually a good place to start to build on the information.

Students have a variety of mental contexts to choose from when searching their memories to relate to the topic at hand. The mental contexts a student selects that can expand on the concept definition under study include constructs that have to be accurate in scholarly or academic definition, but they do not have to be based in reality. It has been long argued by some scholars that most people live inside their heads with limited contact to the outside world, meaning that people live, experience, and process information living in their own mental contexts (worlds), and can make sense of new information and apply it correctly by using existing constructs whether their experience was real or not. For example, a dream is a mental construct; it is not real, but can be used to expand the understanding of a real concept being learned. In the end, the concept definition in the dream must be accurate as per the academic instruction, but the setting or application in which to explain or understand that definition is not held to those standards.

Creative visualization and imagination is a cognitive process of purposefully generating mental imagery either to look back into the past or to look toward the future to manifest something desired. In LEP learning constructing mental images through the use of imagination and creative visualization to trigger the right experience that will relate and expand the concept definition is not only recommended but encouraged. An act of visualization may consist of any mental construct that allows students' play of thought that expand accurate concept definitions in various and personal ways through visualizations or the imagination affording the students the opportunity of viewing the concept from several lenses through applications as they play with each imagined visualization of how the concept(s) can be applied. Each creative visualization or imaginative mental context, providing students stay on track, will provide them with an opportunity to form new understanding of the concept and increase their memory retention of the material they are learning in a very unique and personal way.

Because in mental contexts the existence of something is dependent upon the perception of the subject's mind, the variety of information when utilizing the mental context within LEP learning for each student is limitless. Educators should illustrate the best way to use mental contexts to learn information in their courses through examples so students can understand the process and easily tap into their mental context memories to retrieve information they need. Once students begin working with mental contexts they will fully appreciate the role it plays in clarifying their thoughts as they learn relevant concepts. Most students will quickly find it a significant tool for understanding the information under study.

ENVIRONMENTAL CONTEXT TRIGGERS

The world is a learning environment and everything in it can be presented as data ready to be used when needed. People, in general, no matter who they are or what demographic group they belong to, all react and adapt to their environment, learning and forming new memories every minute of the day. In many ways the environment shapes who the person is and how they perceive their own physical setting. Environmental learning affects students' dispositions, attitudes, and very often approaches to new learning and remembering information. Students see the world, think, understand, and remember in varying ways depending on their upbringing but the perception is also formed through their environmental settings and the way in which they they were taught to act, react, interact, and connect to those environments and settings.

Environmental contexts include all things related to nature, science, the universe, and the totality of the person's environmental experiences throughout the span of their lifetime. Students who are innately naturalistic learn best through the environmental context because it includes all things connected to animals, plants, earth, and so on, but all students should be encouraged to use their environmental contexts to trigger memories that can be used for new learning. Additionally, the environmental context includes surroundings and the person's physical upbringing and attachment to places and things along with emotions and opinions associated with those settings. Surroundings such as the person's habitat, home life, work, school, general environment, family living, and environmental factors such as cultural traditions, ethnic beliefs, values, religion, law and order, courts, societal and social relationships (see figure 6.4), and so on play a role in how new information will be connected to form new knowledge as learned through the environmental context lens.

Scholars agree that environmental experiences, particularly the culture of students, is a significant factor in academic success and should be used wherever and whenever possible for student learning and retention of information. Gay (2000, p. 31) termed "culturally responsive instruction as the process of using the cultural knowledge,

Figure 6.4 LEP Environmental Context

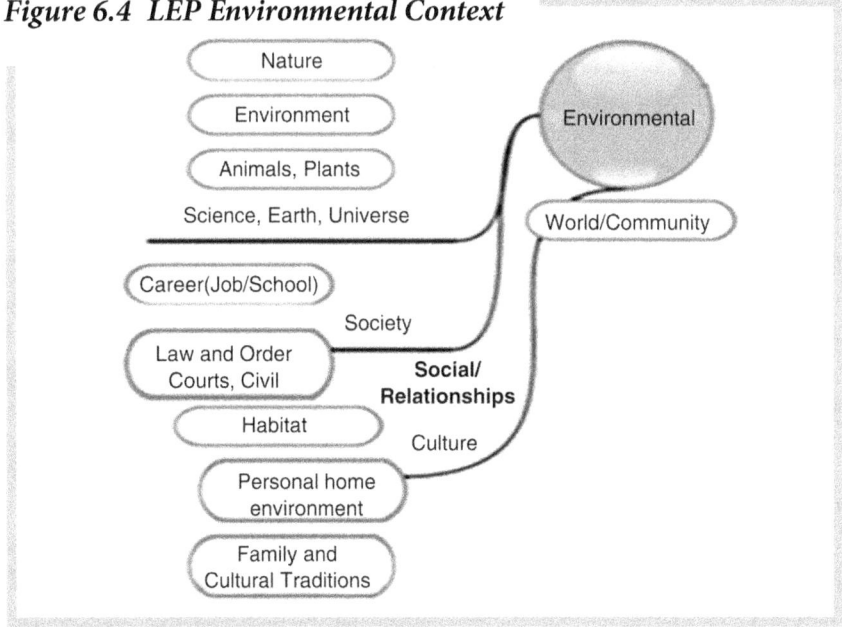

prior experiences, and performance styles of diverse students to make learning more appropriate and effective for them." By using the students' own environmental experiences, values, and perspectives to teach them new material they can construct relationships between themselves and the concepts they are learning and expand that knowledge in a personal way. The personal connection also allows for the creation of a stronger memory trigger to retrieve that information when needed.

Environmental memory is common to all human beings because it resides in the everyday lived experiences within the students as people of the earth, nature, the universe as a whole, and science, and is rooted in social and cultural aspects of people's lives. Using environmental contexts as an active personal learning process intended to expand academic knowledge and habits of inquiry by using inquisitive reflection from the environmental context lens to explain concepts under study offers students the opportunity to use aspects such as culture and social situations as resources for new learning and remembering. This empowers and transforms the students' academic experience because in this format personal knowledge becomes a valuable tool for new learning and they see the value their own personal experience can bring to current and future learning.

PERSONAL BELIEF CONTEXT TRIGGERS

Personal beliefs ignite human perception and have a powerful influence on people. Powerful effects tend to be easily recalled thus personal belief systems should be utilized to learn new information whenever appropriate. People's belief systems are extremely important to LEP learning because they form grids for every facet, every dimension of the students' life and how they perceive every context in their world, which ultimately results in substantial information available for the student to use, frame and explain new knowledge.

LEP personal belief contexts are powerful and usually come in the form of spiritual teachings, universal teachings, and/or religious or personally ingrained beliefs. LEP personal beliefs contexts differ from the LEP spiritual attributes because although they both include spirituality, only personal beliefs include atheism, or rather a disbelief in the existence of any deity. Students who perceive their world from their personal belief spectrum usually include the practice of formalized religion, and universal collective consciousness as a support system. Spirituality often is related to formalized religion, but it is not a requirement, and for the purposes of this book it is not relevant, as the interest lies in the experiences of spirituality as a belief system and how its influence can be connected and shape new information for better concept understanding.

Figure 6.5 LEP Personal Belief Contexts

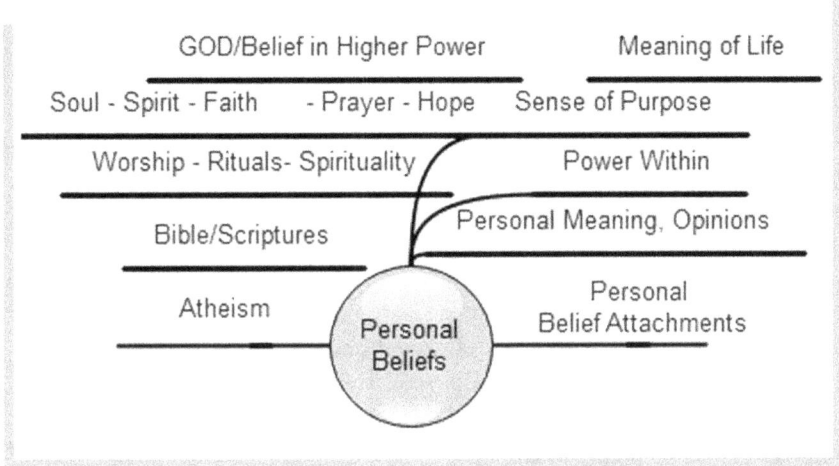

Personal belief contexts are formed through many venues. For example, they include elements such as belief in a higher power, hope, faith, prayer, spirituality, soul, divine love, infinity, ethics, integrity, truth, honesty, religion and so on. Moreover, personal belief contexts are aligned with metaphysical beliefs and analogies, and all personal belief system that the individual possesses. All these ideas may be vastly different from each other, but they all represent various paths of thought, beliefs, and roads that consent to a leap of faith. Even the lack of a belief system in something is a belief system that can be used to connect to material learned for concept understanding and expansion. Thus, students are equipped with a tremendous amount of resources through the personal belief contexts to learn and remember new information in uniquely personal ways.

Personal beliefs are important and can be used as a tool for learning and remembering information because they shape the way in which students perceive, learn, process and remember information. Personal beliefs rooted in traditions and rituals such as various religious practices stemming from many outside sources such as the Bible, Scripture, religious leaders, media and any other external source of exposure turn experience into knowledge that is ripe to be used in the students' current and future learning. Personal beliefs that are based in external sources are in direct contrast to spiritual attributes where students are guided by their spiritually formed attributes from an inward soul level, without outside influence or interference. However, they are just as potent as the end result is not focused in internal or external domains of the experience but the relationship between the information being learned and the memory that will serve to expand its definitions. Meaning the only importance lies in how the experience was registered in their brain and how can serve new knowledge. Where and from what category the information originated was not a factor.

It has been the LEP teaching experience that students' knowledge is based in their personal life's beliefs and experiences in relationship to themselves and others. Thus, this is where LEP starts to build more knowledge to create wisdom, by expanding existing knowledge to include new information but in a uniquely personal way. Given the diversity of classroom it is not possible for educators to connect the material to each of their students, but they can form a relationship between the concept and the students' life and connect material to their beliefs systems allowing each student to explain the concept in and on their own terms. Moreover, using LEP personal belief contexts in the classroom can vastly expand concepts definitions and its application/s and encourage class discussions about students' personal beliefs and their influence on learning.

MORAL CONTEXT TRIGGERS

Although morals and morality are different, they reflect the same characteristics of right and wrong. When a person lives by the moral code, meaning they have morals, they know the difference between right and wrong. In the LEP moral context trigger category, a belief system in a God, higher consciousness or any divine Being, or practicing any form of ritual traditions or religion is not necessary. Morality in an individual is reflected in his or her disposition to do right things, at all times, even if the right thing is challenging or dangerous. The very willingness to do the right thing is a sign of strong ethics. This memory of the strength shown by the individual to do the right thing in various life situations is a life's lesson that can be used for current and future learning.

Honesty, truthfulness, sincerity, integrity, and truth are moral principles. Memories stemming from the person's inner ethical structure that includes these principles are also associated with their conscience. Information from the moral conscience context may derive from the person's perceived views of the justices or injustices in their culture, spirit, society, government, or religious aspects (see figure 6.6). But it may also be pulled from the memories of the self, their inner secret places that governed their behavior and and life choices.

Moral values although often interpreted differently by different people are highly important to some students because they are connected to character. Generally, students high in moral character are living their life by a moral direction, a compass,

Figure 6.6 LEP Moral Contexts

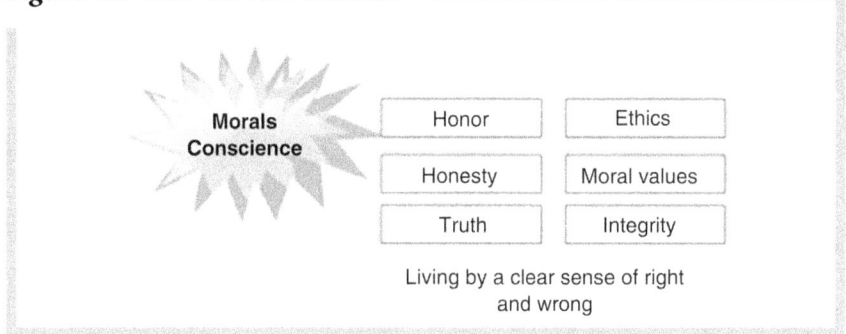

that is aligned truth and integrity. They are governed by ethical and moral principles, that guide their experiences in life.

A conscience can be a strong memory trigger that can assist in framing new information from a very internal and personal perspective. A conscience is an inner voice/sense that acts as a guide within the person, impelling the individual toward the right, rather than wrong, course of action. Often this can be seen as a rigid disciplined structure shaped by an immovable sense judgment by people who are subscribing to a particular standard. But the students who live by their perceived moral values and codes relish the clear sense of "what is right and what is wrong" and are committed to living and interpreting the world from that perspective. Experiences from the moral context can be a valuable source of information that students have access to that can be used to form new understanding, and educators should encourage students to tap into the moral context whenever appropriate to use as a resource to frame new information for better understanding and application(s).

In summary, the LEP context trigger categories provide students emotional, physical, mental, moral, environmental, and personal belief contexts to utilize when memories need to be triggered to explain and frame new information for comprehension and application purposes. If memories cannot be accessed or are not available, students must switch to the imagination and play with the various imagined contexts being careful to hold the true academic concept definition in mind until the right fit is found. Contexts can also be used in combination with each other to clarify or to frame new information to the best understanding of the students. Often this may need several contextual lenses to find the most accurate information that will explain the concept to the fullest potential. Educators should encourage students to practice learning new information through their existing context memories, and as always should take time to modify and adjust the LEP context worksheets to better suit the course and student needs.

CHAPTER SEVEN

LEP Memory Hacks

> LEP Memory Hacks
> LEP Trigger Categories
> LEP Sensory Memory Triggers
> LEP Attribute Triggers
> LEP Context Triggers

CREATING LEP MEMORY HACKS USING TRIGGER CATEGORIES

While LEP memory triggers assist students to connect to information to explain or expand its properties, memory hacks cue the triggered information for retrieval and boost long-term retention of information. Both LEP memory triggers and memory hacks are equally effective in their prescribed rolls because of the personal nature in which the information is learned, and are very powerful in learning and retrieving information when combined together. Once students understand and are comfortable with how to work with memory triggers to retrieve existing information from their minds' databases to explain new concepts through their sensory memories, LEP learning attributes, and/or the LEP contexts, they are ready to create memory hacks using the same classifications to retrieve the information from their long-term memory when needed.

LEP teaching methods focus on learning information from a personal point of view. Research indicates that people remember things better and retain them longer when they associate meaning to them. The more personal the meaning, the stronger the memory retention and recall. The memory when retrieved is not an exact reproduction of the experience; researchers at McGill University indicate that every time a person recalls a memory, the brain has to rebuild that memory in order to restore it; thus, in this process, memories are often inadvertently changed or modified from their original schemas. The truth behind the memory of the experiences are not central to the learning process; as long as the representations of the memories are correct for the concept definitions and applications, they can be used as a memory hack.

However, the memory hacks the students select to retrieve the information they need must have proper strength to be used as a cue for memory retrieval later, as it is the action behind the word that brings information forward to be recalled. McKenzie Wark (2004) interpreted a hack as "an action applicable to any creative act. . .to abstract. . . to produce the plane upon which different things may enter into relation." In the case of LEP learning, it is in relation to remembering concepts being learned, as creating strong memory hacks relative to the concept under study will greatly aid in the retrieval of that information when needed. Shook (2017) describes the function of a hack as "to break apart collective memory's seemingly fixed narratives, allowing multiple stories to emerge into actual life." The use of personal information through the individual's own perceptual stories, which triggered a connection between the student's existing memories and information being remembered, allows for great freedom in creating strong memory hacks that will easily retrieve the learned information when needed.

Creating LEP memory hacks to cue the brain to retrieve learned information is effective because the students are deliberately hacking earlier formed connections that were established in their mind from a personal perspective when learning that information. Another effective strategy that accompanies remembering and retrieving of information through LEP memory hacks is the visual organization of information. The organization of information is always important, but LEP stresses organization in a visual and symbolic way, adding images to all notes as a way to reinforce memory cues.

Patterns of organization such as chronological, sequence, cause and effect, problem and solution, or compare and contrast are just some of the ways the information can be organized visually to create strong memory hacks. Educators are always encouraged to include their own organizational methods but must always ensure that images are included in the equation. The selected organization pattern that will help with arranging the information and create memory hacks will depend on the students' preference and the topic under study.

As with other aspects of LEP teaching and learning, educators must dedicate hands-on practical time in class to ensure students understand and know how to create LEP memory hacks using sensory memory triggers, LEP trigger attributes, and LEP trigger contexts and record information using the personal memory design hacks patterns (activity) to cue and retrieve information. Using the LEP personal memory hack design worksheets will be very helpful to students as the textual information along with the image of the memory hack will assist in sending appropriate signals to the brain to retrieve the correct information.

Creating LEP Memory Hacks Using Sensory Triggers

Just as sensory memory is used to create triggers to connect the existing information to new knowledge for clarity and examples of how the information can be applied to real life, sensory memory is used to create memory hacks to cue the learned information. Sensory memory, as mentioned in the earlier chapters, includes the five senses of vision, hearing, touch, smell, and taste, and in the form of a created sensory memory hack can cue any triggered memory relative to the concept. Drawing on their strongest "sense" or a combination of "senses," students select the sensory experience from their triggered memories to create a memory hack to cue the information when needed. Once a memory hack is formed, its description or image, if encoded properly, can be an enduring means to cue information about the concept and retrieved at will.

Will it be sound? Sight? Touch? Any sense the students select in which to remember the concept is correct if it expands concept definition. It is important to encourage students to play with each sense, use varied scenarios with the senses, and have fun working with the memory cues to create the best hack relative to concept as possible. The longer the student spends time in "play" trying to create sensory experience hacks, the higher the chances of long-term memory retention of the new information.

Once a memory is triggered and the students have an understanding of the concept, the students select the best memory hack that will cue the information that needs to be recalled. In order to stay organized students should complete the LEP sensory memory hack activity for each concept they need to remember by writing down the information in the appropriate boxes and include the memory hack image that will be used to cue the retrieval of the information. It is important that the memory hack is presented not only in written and diagram formats but also in an image form. Images and snapshots are usually much easier to remember, recall, and retrieve and serve as strong visual memory reinforcements in learning.

Creating LEP Memory Hacks Using Attribute Triggers

In addition to sensory memories, students may use their LEP learning attributes to create strong memory hacks. Memory hacks to cue learned information from triggered memories through the lens of learning attributes such as linguistic, logical, naturalistic, spiritual, interpersonal, intrapersonal, musical, or existential attributes or even conditioned responses increases the chances of long-term retention because of their personal approach to learning the material.

Although learning to create LEP memory hacks is a simple mental exercise, most student learn best through example. Thus, some class time on the onset of the course should be devoted to reviewing how students can use their triggered memories from their various attributes as related to the concepts learned to create memory hacks as cues to recall that information. For example, reviewing various learning attributes with students, and offering the educators' personal illustrations on some of the ways the educators cue their brains to receive information through a particular attribute as it related to the topic at hand, will guide and instruct students toward the correct way to tap into these innate attributes to create their own memory hacks to use as cues to retrieve learned information.

The optimal way for students to create a memory hack as a cue to retrieve learned information using the LEP learning attributes is to align themselves with their strongest attribute that is most suited to the information that must be cued. Students who are linguistic, and who can innately speak, read, and write well; like to play with language and like word games; or even like to give speeches or performances, should be encouraged to create their memory hacks as cues relative to the information they are learning based on their love of language. Using the verbal-linguistic memory hack gives students a tool to retrieve information that they need and an opportunity to model their affinity for language, which will increase their long-term memory retention.

Students who are logical or strong with numbers can use their analytical experiences, understanding of formulas and numbers, and logical thinking processes as memory hacks to cue information when needed. Their preference for problem solving, and a more scientific approach to life, can garnish them a vast pool of knowledge they can tap into to create memory hacks that relate to the information they are learning. Any complex and abstract ideas that include the reasoning approach, conceptualizing relationship between things, and so on would be ideal tools for the logical student to utilize in creating memory hacks that can cue information from triggered memories.

Learning through music has been a learning modality accepted by many scholars because of the positive end results music can offer in terms of increased memory retention. Outside of the general benefits that music can provide in learning such as learning of vocabulary, and enhancing listening skills, playing with musical instruments can present experiences in pitch, timbre, or texture. Music experiences hold, invite, and incite feelings and experiences that can be used to cue information.

Musical and rhythmic students are usually innately strong in aural skills and generally will be able to create memory hacks relative to what they are studying by their experiences through hearing sound, music, rhythm, and so. Many students feel, learn, and understand their world through music and rhythm but these students understand the relationship between sounds, which can also invoke strong emotions, that can be used to create memory hacks to retrieve appropriate information. Musical students should be encouraged to use musical information as cues to create their memory hacks to retrieve the learned information because they thrive within the environment of music and often see, learn and perceive the world from this perspective.

Intrapersonal attributes possess an internalized version of the attributes of interpersonal attributes. Intrapersonal students are self-motivated and inner reflective and are aware of how they affect the world around them. Their solitary introspective approach to life also transcends into how they also like to learn and remember information. Usually intrapersonal students recognize their strengths and weaknesses and can draw upon that knowledge for future learning. Because intrapersonal students are introspective and can reflect on past events, decisions, and actions and analyze them in different ways, they can easily use triggered memories of these types of experiences as cues to create memory hacks to retrieve the learned information when they need it.

According to Gardner (1993, p. 42), "Interpersonal intelligence is the core capacity to notice distinctions among others, particularly contrasts in their moods, temperaments, motivations and intentions." By this statement the assumption is that interpersonal students communicate effectively, show empathy, and are focused more on others than on themselves. Gardner, (1993) also suggests that interpersonal students also prefer to work in teams, or groups, and have a more collaborative approach to life and learning. Interpersonal students understand people and exhibit strong relationships with others, thus forming meaningful experiences that could be used as strong cues to retrieved learned knowledge.

Interpersonal learning just as intrapersonal learning is basically personal learning from an innate characteristically preferential mode. Since interpersonal students are skilled at managing relationships and negotiation, these students will flourish brainstorming personal memory hacks as cues relative to the concepts learned through more social systems. Interpersonal memory hacks are one of the strongest hacks available to students because memories with others can hold significant meaning, which often is retained for the long-term and retrieved easily when needed.

Naturalistic cues can create very strong memory hacks. Naturalistic students are able to see patterns and feel a deep connection with their environment and surroundings. These students are sensitive and have an empathy for nature, plants, and animals, and all these experiences can be used to create memory hacks that will cue the needed information when desired. Naturalistic students enjoy exploring and perceiving their world from the natural phenomenon and learning from that perspective. Thus, this innate strength is ideal to utilize in creating memory hacks to retrieve learned information. Naturalist students should be encouraged by educators to create memory hacks that are strongly connected to their triggered experiences and environment rooted in nature as related to the concepts that were learned to best cue the information when needed.

Since everyday and spiritual thinking come from the same processes, it is only in the perception of the meaning behind the thoughts that the difference is found. Students approaching learning through the spiritual lens have a unique perspective on the way their experiences are triggered and relate to the information they are learning. The students in the spiritual sphere perceive through spiritual senses working with the inner rather than outer perspectives to learn and remember information. The more spiritual data they accumulate through their representation of reality, the more information they have available that could trigger existing memories when they are learning, and the more data they have accessible to use as memory hacks to retrieve those rich set of inputs. Educators should encourage all students to examine their own spiritual depth perceptions and relevant learning and utilize the spiritual attribute as a memory hack to retrieve information when appropriate.

Existential students also have a large database of memories they can utilize to create memory hacks to cue information for retrieval. Existential students are more focused on global, worldly views. These students have usually spent much time and questioned the meaning of life, human existence, and cosmic functions, and can use these triggered memories as they relate to the concepts under study to create formidable memory hacks to cue learned information. Allowing the richness of existential experiences and forming memory hacks from this global perspective allows students to be open and nonjudgmental, and view life from different angles. These fresh perspectives could be used as potent cues for memory retention and retrieval of relevant information.

Conditioned responses manifest through patterns in people's life. The range of automatic responses once consciously thought about is limitless, and all can be used as a source for learning and memory retention. Conditioned responses are valuable cues for the creation of memory hacks because they infuse the knowledge of whole human systems of physiological, emotional, and behavioral memories, which can contribute significantly to creating appropriate memory hacks to various topics to retrieve information.

Creating Memory Hacks Using LEP Trigger Contexts

Life's journey provides numerous experiences in various contexts that form our memories and can be used as cues to create memory hacks to recall learned information. LEP contexts include physical, environmental, emotional, mental, personal beliefs and moral contexts that all students have at their disposal to easily remember and recall information. The symbolism of the LEP tree (as seen in activity), which includes unlimited branches that stem from the bole of the tree extending into different contextual areas, offers students a visual illustration of the unlimited choices from the various contexts they can draw from when searching for the most suited memory hack that can cue the correct information whenever it is desired.

Each experience regardless of context that touches the individual is registered in the brain and may be available to be recalled at will with the right memory hack to cue the information. A wide range of encounters, observations, and perceptions of the totality of the individuals' experiences through each LEP context provide data that students can use to create memory hacks to cue learned knowledge. Whether it is the physical, environmental, emotional, mental, a personal belief or moral context or whether it is used in different combinations with each other, memories from these experiences offer different types of recollections that are distinct and can be reconstructed to be used as a cue to create a memory hack.

In the physical context, biological cues can serve as memory hacks based in bodily behaviors, functions, and reactions because biological aspects often can create intense experiences. Biological contexts include genetics, physiology, and all physical aspects, illness, wellness, energy levels, reproductivity, pain, sexuality, metabolism, and so on. Activities, sports, exercise, and physical engagements also invite the body into the learning and remembering space and as such offer the body to the students as a memory tool for new learning. Physical/biological conditions are necessary for human beings to learn and understand how their body and organism function, and these conditions can be prime to remember and recall new information.

Body consciousness and awareness are effective tools for memory retention and retrieval of information. Remembering information that has to be recalled later through the physical lens allows students to use various memories or characterization of their bodily experiences relative to the concepts learned to create memory hacks to cue information when needed. Biological pathways often lead to creating strong memory hacks because students' knowledge of their body and its experiences is vast, and the topic of their body usually holds their interest and engages them in the material, which ultimately helps with long-term memory retention and retrieval of information through the created memory hack.

The environmental context is also a lucrative field that can be used as cues to create strong memory hacks to retrieve information because of the enormous amount of developmental data that it holds. Environmental context refers to aspects of a person's setting and surroundings in every form and every situation at every stage in their life. Environmental aspects also include factors within the environment such as nature, animals, plants, earth, universe, and so on and include world communities, laws, culture, family, work, school, societal norms, and even lessons and growth that occurred as a result of the person's environment.

Environmental contexts are especially a fertile ground for the creation of memory hacks in retrieving learned material because those experiences tend to form behaviors and perceptions from childhood on; throughout that time, much occurs and is registered in the long-term memory. This pool of information can be used as a cue to create a memory hacks to retrieve needed information. Creating a memory hack from the environmental context is really reusing, recycling, rethinking, and reprocessing the existing information to use as a cue to create a strong memory hack so that it may be retrieved at will.

In addition to the already mentioned physical and environmental contexts, emotional contexts are also important in an individual's life and can be used to create formidable memory hacks. Research suggests that emotions and feelings are key factors for effective transformation (Dirkx, 2006). Lawrence (2008) indicated that the activation of sensory and imagery cognitive processes can allow the construction of fresh points of view and interconnection with other dimensions of cognition. This means that emotional contexts hold valuable information that is malleable but can be used as cues to hack existing information in the brain for easy retrieval. Brookfield (2002) suggests that students should challenge their own emotions and feelings (LEP learning encourages students to work with their emotions and feelings as much as possible as cues for memory retention of learned material) as they are an important piece of the meaning-making process that underlies the unconscious forms associated with learning (Dirkx, 2006) and memory retention.

Feelings are mental connections and reactions to emotions. Feelings are learned behaviors that are usually triggered by an external incident. They are a subjective energy that is influenced by every human being's personal perspective of the experience, their beliefs, and existing memories, and as such are distinctly creative tools to use as cues to create memory hacks to recall information.

Emotions evoke feelings. Feelings assign meaning to emotions because they are the next thing that occurs after a person has an emotion. Unlike feelings, which are unique and rooted in perceptions of people and can vary greatly, emotions, while they may vary slightly individually, and depending on the situation, are generally universally similar across all people. For example, seeing a baby smile usually causes the same emotional responses of a smile in return regardless of belief systems. Thus, students may use this emotional context state with its wide range of both positive and negative experiences of emotions and feelings as a great source of knowledge that can be triggered to connect to concepts and that can be used to create memory hacks as cues to remember and retrieve the learned information later.

Likewise, LEP personal belief context hacks can be of great service to students when trying to remember learned information. Personal beliefs, and personal association with a higher power, inner faith, and growing with a sense of purpose other than materialistic views, soul connections, and so on often is firmly rooted in students' experiences and the way they perceive the world. This internal world of spiritual contexts offers a a store house of information that students can use as memory hacks to remember information in a very personal way.

Students using the LEP personal belief contexts to create memory hacks to remember new information generally activate their spirit, or higher self, as they learn and perceive information from that spiritual or universal lens. They see the experience from an inner perspective; thus, they are strongly encouraged to use their faith, values, and personal belief systems, regardless of what they are, to create memory hacks to retrieve learned information from their memory storage when they need it. Many students are deeply connected to their spiritual, religious, or universal beliefs because the memories are personally meaningful to them; thus, their potency to be used as memory hack tools increases.

Creating memory hacks using these deep inner experiences opens doors to an expansive world of possibilities and opportunities to remember concepts learned through a more holistic approach using students' inner personal belief systems. Many times, thoughts and ideas occur in the context of benevolence, and can be understood and remembered through that perceptual lens. Moreover, using memory hacks from the spiritual/universal/religious category often suspends logic, which allows students to be much more creative when selecting memory hacks to cue the remembered information.

Mental contexts are important aspects of the human cognition and condition. Mental contexts are various states of knowledge, judgments, reasoning, assessments, opinions, suppositions, or perceptions that may or may not change over the lifespan of the individual. The mental contexts usually include, but are certainly not limited to, thoughts, ideas, visualizations, motivations, habits, perceptions, intelligence, logic, rational and irrational thinking, nostalgia, and so on—anything that is constructed within the students' minds.

Mental contexts offer students a wide range of cognitive experiences that can be used as cues to create memory hacks. Mental contexts are not directly observable, but they are very powerful. Max Planck, the German quantum theorist and Nobel Prize winner, stated that "when you change the way you look at things, the things you look at changes." Thus, the understanding and the significance of something, and whether it is retained for future use, is registered on a mental plane and if we change the way we look at a concept, the concept will become alive in another way.

Mental contexts are malleable, ready to be molded to form new interpretations or developed into memory hacks to recall the learned information while still maintaining the integrity of the information. The ability of the mental contexts, which assists students to rapidly shift in response to any experience and create new memories, new constructs in the form of cues to create memory hacks to retrieve information, is ideally suited to be used with LEP memory retention and retrieval of information. One of the reasons is that the human cognitive database expands with each piece of knowledge, creating new wisdom; in this case, it will create a cue in the form of a memory hack to expand knowledge while simultaneously retrieve the desired information. In the mental context realm, everything begins and ends as an activity of the consciousness and all information can be used to create distinctive memory hacks to retrieve any learned information.

Moral contexts were an important addition to learning and remembering with LEP because these contexts bind human thinking about how they live and perceive their world.

Moral contexts can be subjective, as the very word suggests layers and layers of definitions all depending on with which lens the word "moral" is viewed. But in LEP teaching and learning, a moral context is a perception of viewing information from a set of personal moral codes of ethics, integrity, honor, and truth, which conform at least somewhat to society's and community's lawful standards. Thus, LEP learning views exhibiting moral values in a generic sharing kind of form.

Moral thinking and contexts that shape moral qualities such as an awareness of a conscience and the person's responsibility to others as another human being and so on are ideal to be utilized as memory hacks to retrieve information. Working with existing information from the moral context lens in trying to create cues from the person's inner ethical structure and conscience can create strong and very memorable memory hacks that can be used when necessary information needs to be recalled. People with a stellar moral compass and strong ethics reflect the characteristics of knowing right from wrong, honesty, truthfulness, sincerity, integrity, and most importantly truth, and can easily use these qualities as cues to form memory hacks for learned information whenever appropriate.

Regardless of which method is chosen, sensory triggers, LEP learning attributes, or the LEP contexts or whether the students used "real" memories or "imagined" to create a memory hack to cue the existing information in the brain, the process will boost the memory retention of the information learned. Students will realize that the tools they need to remember the information they are learning are there; they are just not always accessing it to use this information in different or the best ways. By continuing to use memory hacks to reinforce and easily retrieve information through the use of personal applications of sensory triggers, LEP learning attributes, and/or the LEP contexts, students will significantly increase their learning outcomes and enjoy the learning process because of the personal connection to the information learned and vastly improve their memory retention of information in the long term.

CHAPTER EIGHT

LEP Personal Memory Design Patterns

Organizing Information Visually through
Organizational Design Patterns
Chronological Pattern
Sequence Pattern
Cause-and-Effect Pattern
Problem-and-Solution Pattern
Compare-and-Contrast Pattern

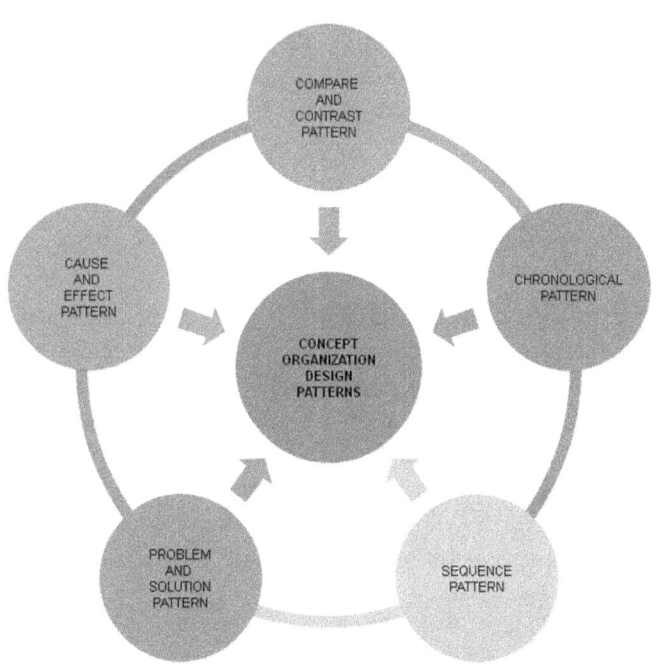

Students seek out organizational patterns to help them make sense of information. Organizing information through a personal memory design pattern greatly assists students in making sense of information and assists in memory retention of learned material. The organization of information is a necessary function that allows students to easily navigate through enormous amounts of notes to find the content that they need. Notes become study guides; thus, when working with a substantial amount of information, a clear path to find what is looked for is a must or the information will just be words on paper and will be deemed as having little value. It is challenging to focus on learning and memory retention of information if students spend most of their time organizing the overwhelming amount of notes they have taken before they even begin the studying process.

Most students know that preparing for tests requires more than just memorizing information. Often, they have to demonstrate critical thinking skills, which is much more than just memorizing of material; thus, visual organization through a personal memory design pattern to see related concepts and to make meaningful connections to the information is imperative. LEP personal design patterns of organizing information are based on the common patterns of organization used by students such as, chronological, sequence, cause and effect, problem and solution and compare and contrast, but they are also distinctively unique because they not only hold information gained from lecture notes, or other resources such as a textbook, but also include the memory trigger used to connect to the new information and the memory hack used to recall that information. In this way the knowledge is visually organized in an academic but personal way with symbolic memory hacks included to retrieve that knowledge when needed.

ORGANIZING INFORMATION VISUALLY THROUGH ORGANIZATIONAL DESIGN PATTERNS

There are many ways to organize information, but the LEP personal memory design patterns are visual organizers that use the five common text structures of chronological, sequence, cause and effect, problem and solution, and compare and contrast to assist in visual organization of information for the purposes of easier comprehension and easy information retrieval. The structures within the design patterns are equally effective in defining and reinforcing information. The organization of ideas and thoughts relative to the concept learned, which includes visual representation(s) of the memory hack, creates a stronger memory recall when the information is needed.

The best way to visually organize and categorize information for best memory recall will vary depending on the content under study and the students' preference.

Students should practice using the various personal design patterns as blueprints for future learning, as clear organization of information enhances the ease with which the students can understand and remember the information. Using personal memory designs to visually organize information mentioned in this book will keep students on target with information gathering and organization and will boost memory retention levels. Educators should make their own recommendations as to what kind of personal memory design patterns for organizing information will work best for their courses and students.

Chronological Design Pattern of Organization

Chronological patterns of organization arrange information according to a progression of time. It is timeline thinking, which can move backward or forward. Mapping the content chronologically usually entails moving through the timeline of events by using the before or after pattern. When students are working with chronological organizations of information to take notes, they should have a strong sense of chronology, meaning a knowing of when events occurred and in what temporal order to investigate relationships between their existing memories relative to the concept and new information learned.

Often a concept is best understood and remembered through various segments of time such as concepts with a historical nature. However, often students have a difficult time remembering in a chronological order. It is hard to decipher for them whether an event happened a month ago, 6 months ago, or a year ago. At those times students refer back to lived experienced memories they can connect to that marked their chronological existence, such as "Well I didn't have the cat then, so it must have been 6 months ago."

The function of memory is not only to record the past but also to reconstruct it when summoned according to the requirements of the needs of the present. Using seasons and special occasions like anniversaries, birthdays, and so on can effectively mark time, all of which can helps students organize information they need to remember through chronological patterns using lived experiences. When using chronological patterns, each section represents a segment of time, and the subpoints in each section of time discuss significant concepts, their meaning, and connections that occurred during that time. This includes all triggered memories as related to the concept. It is especially important to remind students that sketching or inserting an image of the memory hack in the chronological worksheet will greatly increase their memory retention of concept information. Educators are encouraged to design their own chronological activities to suit their course needs or educator preferences. Students may also create their own chronological mind map that fits their vision of how they wish to record the information (see figure 8.1).

Figure 8.1 LEP Chronological Organizational Pattern

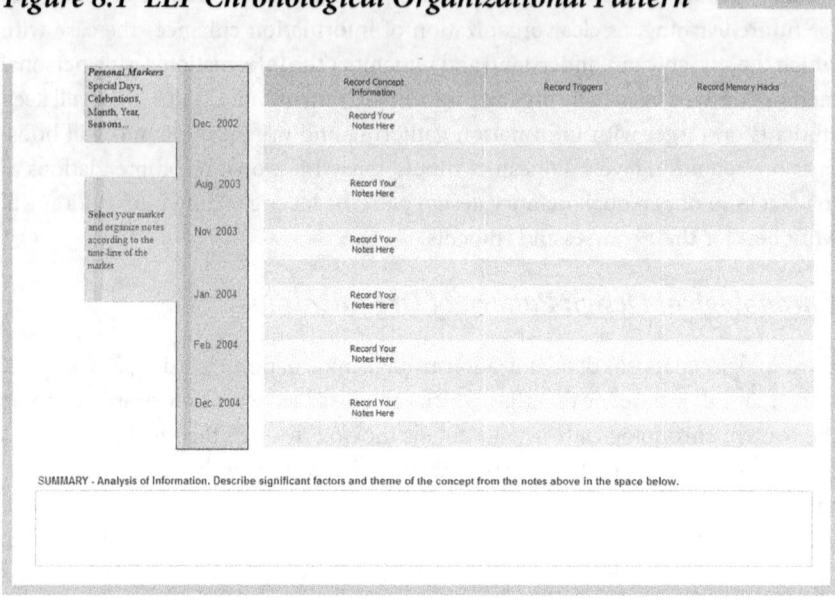

Sequence Design Pattern of Organization

Sequence patterns of organization differ from the chronological timeline because it is not always time but rather the order of importance that something happened that may be of priority to the individual. When students sequence information, they arrange it to follow a particular, logical order or a recurrent pattern that makes sense to them. Taking notes and creating a memory hack using sequence to remember and retrieve certain information may be the best choice for the student or the content under study. Sequence assists learning and memory retention because it places new information in the students' mind in a specific way (in sequence of something they already know and make sense of), which makes it easier to understand, learn, and recall later.

In sequencing, the students should focus on organizing their information using the first, next, then, and ending with finally sequence, organizational pattern as identification markers in explaining and remembering the content under study. Memory triggers and memory hacks must always be included when sequencing organization of information, as their visual effects will greatly increase the long-term memory of information and offer students a tool to retrieve that information as needed. Worksheets (see figure 8.2) to visually demonstrate the processes of sequencing for

Figure 8.2 LEP Sequence Design Pattern

It is important to remember that sequence may mean "order of importance" not necessarily "time" as in the chronological order of events

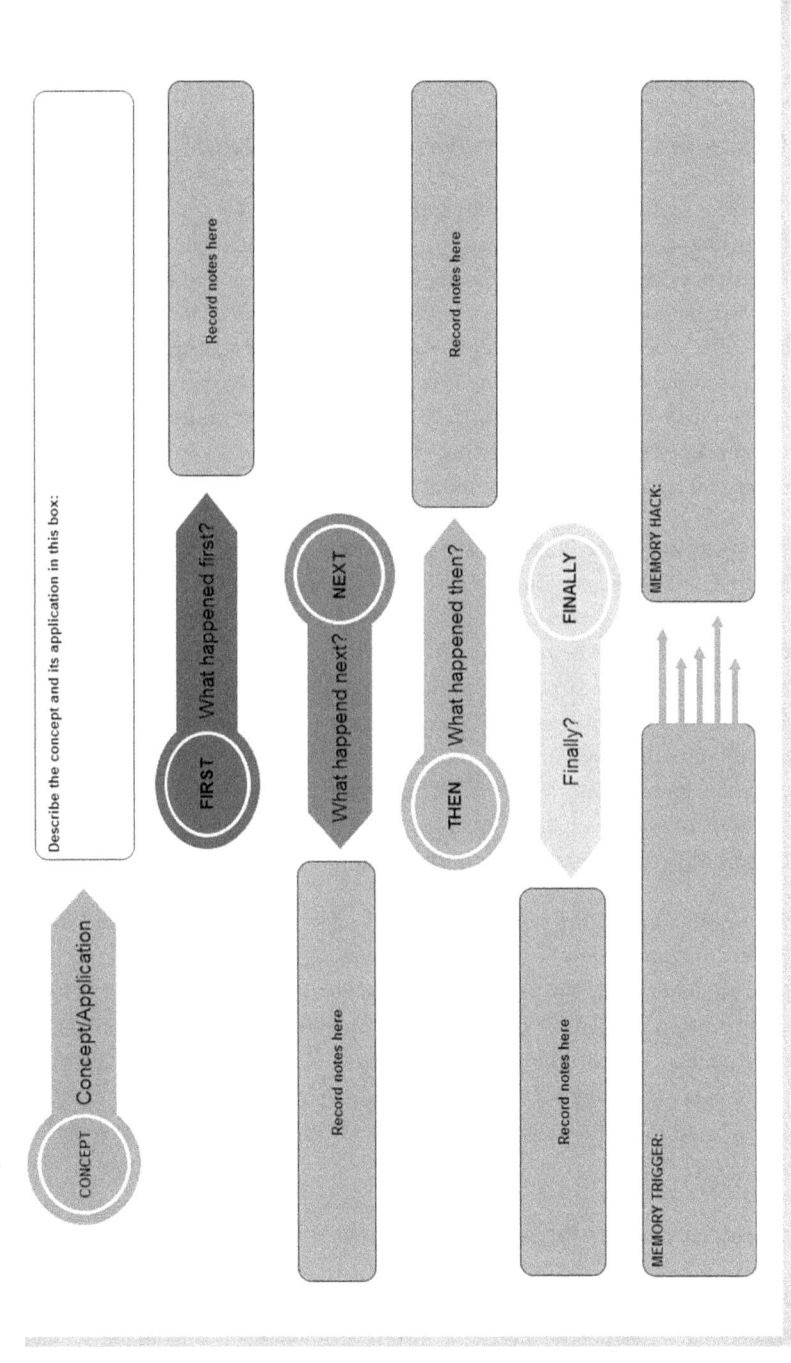

CHAPTER EIGHT LEP PERSONAL MEMORY DESIGN PATTERNS

the purposes of organizing the information for memory hacks should be available to students both in traditional courses and online. As always, the worksheets are deliberately kept simple so that the educator could modify all activities to meet the needs of the course and students.

Cause-and-Effect Design Pattern of Organization

The cause-and-effect pattern of organizing information is very valuable in LEP learning because so much of life is learned through the cause-and-effect paradigm and these experiences can expand on existing knowledge. Cause and effect is a relationship between two elements where one results in another. It is a relational action-to-reaction structure between actions, events, people, things, and so on. Students can organize their information and combine it with triggered lived experiences and knowledge learned from those experiences relative to the concept under study and remember the concept definition by creating strong memory hacks to accompany the visual organization of information through the cause-and-effect pattern of organization.

The cause-and-effect pattern of organization is seen as a very valuable tool in the organization of information by LEP teaching methods because it explains reasons why something has occurred, and the effect (action) of what occurred, which is the cause. To simplify, when students are organizing information in the cause-and-effect relationship, the information explains why the "cause" of something happened. Cause-and-effect organization offers students a deeper understanding of the effects of why something has happened or its effects, rather than focusing on the timeline or sequence of events, as in the chronological or sequence order, respectively. The inclusion of memory hacks when organizing notes through the cause-and-effect paradigms will greatly assist in long-term memory retention of the concepts under study.

Educators may use the sample cause-and-effect worksheets included in this book but are encouraged to be creative and develop their own worksheets to better suit their student population and course needs. Figure 8.3 illustrates the LEP cause-and-effect process at a glance. The worksheets were meant to provide a general guideline for students who should also be encouraged to create their own cause-and-effect patterns of organizing their information whether through enlarging or reorganizing space or adding other categories to expand concept understanding and memory retention of the material learned.

Problem-and-Solution Design Pattern of Organization

Problem-and-solution patterns of organization, not to be confused with cause and effect, concern organizing a problem, a dilemma concerning an issue that needs a

Figure 8.3 LEP Cause and Effect Organizational Pattern

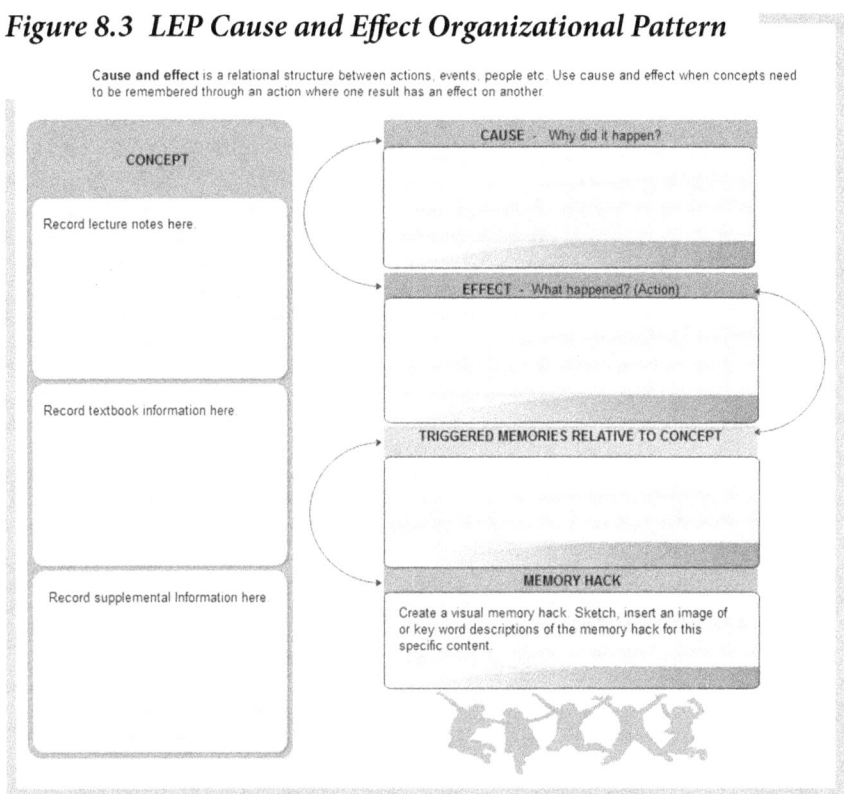

remedy to be solved presented through a visual, organized, and clear way. Cause and effect are limited to describing causes and effects of happenings, but problem-and-solution organizational patterns present a solution to the problem, not just describe why something occurred and its effects. Organizing concepts through this method, allows students to use their lived experience as prior wisdom, and affords them the opportunity to use that knowledge for current and future learning. Students can use the problem itself or the remedies attempted before the solution was found as tools for understanding and organizing information relative to the new concepts learned (see figure 8.4). Traditionally, students strong in the mathematics and sciences area relate well to learning and organization through the process of problem-and-solution patterns. But all students have experienced problems they had to solve in their own lives and this knowledge will assist in creating the problem-and-solution pattern of organization of new information in their current course work.

Students learn through the engagement of real problems and solutions that their authentic experience can generally align the concepts application(s) to

Figure 8.4 LEP Problem and Solution Organizational Pattern

Problem and Solution

Describe the Problem

Steps to Solution

1. _____
2. _____
3. _____

SOLUTION DESCRIPTION

Describe the chosen solution, and how it affects the concepts being learned in this box.

MEMORY TRIGGERS

Describe the memory trigger used to connect to concepts learned to expand concepts definition and applications in this box.

MEMORY HACKS

Describe the memory hack selected to retrieve concept information in this box.

---

their reality. When working with problem-and-solution organizational patterns, students' critical thinking skills increase as they brainstorm remembering all the different problems and how they were resolved that they can relate to the concept under study in their life. Students also use critical thinking skills in considering how to best organize information captured based on the problem-and-solution parameters.

Educators should encourage students to use the problem-and-solution design pattern to organize information whenever appropriate and possible. Generally, the problem-and-solution design pattern divides the information into two main sections: the problem and the solution. However, the inclusion of the LEP memory triggers and memory hacks in organizing new information within the problem-and-solution pattern will greatly assist in adding valuable knowledge that students can use in the concept application process and in the long-term memory of the information.

Compare-and-Contrast Design Pattern of Organization

Comparative thinking is a natural form of thought. From birth children learn to compare and contrast in order to learn. Without the ability to make comparisons and view one element against another to observe similarities and differences, learning would not be possible. Research suggested that while some comparative thinking may be automatic, people also have the cognitive wherewithal to choose comparison that make us happier; this means people choose and select a memory that is most conducive to compare with new information for optimal learning (Kassam, Morewedge, Gilbert, Wilson, & Wilson, 2011).

Rational explanation or the best way to understand and remember information often manifests through compare-and-contrast thought processes. In the case of LEP learning, students select a triggered memory that most relates to the concept they are studying by personally connecting with it and creating a memory hack in which to recall it. By encouraging students to analyze concepts and organize them through the compare-and-contrast approach, and then personally connect to the information, educators strengthen their students' ability to remember the content and assist them to create strong memory hacks in which to retrieve the information when required.

The structure of compare and contrast helps students organize information, which helps them to remember the learned concepts later with greater precision and clarity. When students compare, they estimate, measure, and look for similarities and differences between data or data sets within the same general class in which to organize information (see figure 8.5). By working with their memory triggers to personalize the concepts and applications and creating memory hacks to include in learning and organizing the information process, students are allowed thinking flexibility to apply past knowledge to new situations in a visually organized way. Moreover, focusing student thinking on analyzing a pair of ideas that relate to the concept they are learning and compare and contrast information from a personal

Figure 8.5 LEP Compare and Contrast Organizational Pattern

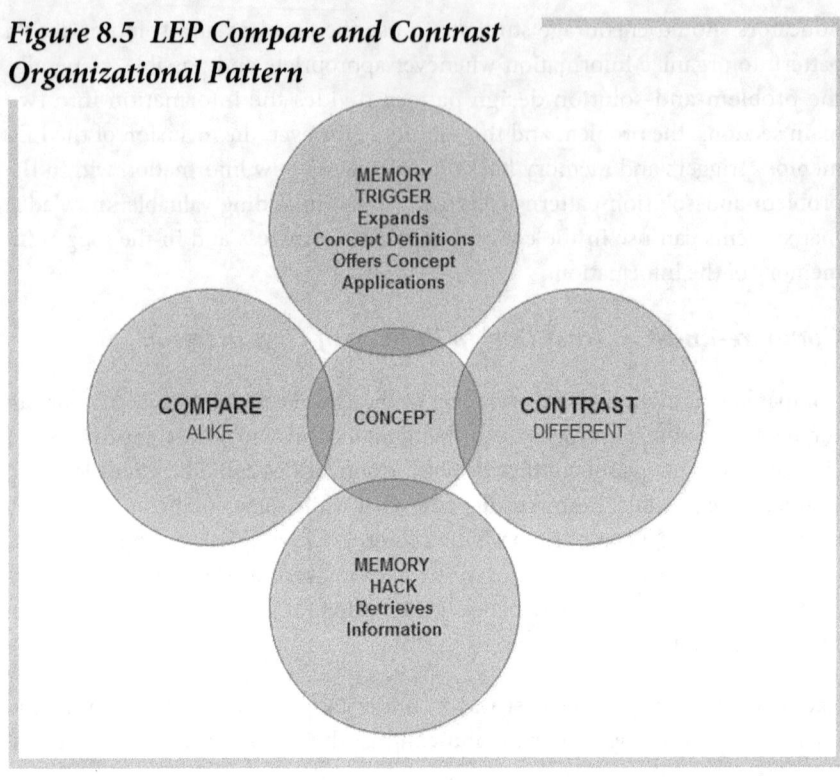

way will help with the concept application process and strengthen memory retention of new information.

LEP teaching methods utilize the following personal memory design patterns to organize information: chronological, sequence, cause and effect, problem and solution, and compare and contrast. Other organizational designs are available for use at the educator's discretion to fit the needs of their courses or students, and all educators are encouraged to explore the best options to suit their requirements. Additionally, LEP vastly improves memory retention of the material learned because it includes memory triggers and memory hacks to be recorded with academic information gained through lectures and textbooks when organizing information to better assist in expanding concept understanding and its application(s) from personal knowledge and perception.

The overwhelming amount of information students are often subjected to demands an organizal design pattern that will make the information captured readable, usable, and well organized. There are many designs to organize information, and each student must select the best design pattern to use with each topic so they can easily understand what is recorded and why. Information about a topic may be infinite; however, with appropriate organizational pattern, the information may be structured in a user-friendly and clear way. Educators are encouraged to practice these diferent designs with students so that they can learn to organize the content for better understanding and memory retention purposes. Showing students the value of organizing information from LEP's personal learning approach will connect students to the information and motivate them to continue the practice on their own and successfully manage the information they are receiving throughout their time in academia.

CHAPTER NINE

IT'S PERSONAL: REFRAMING EDUCATION THROUGH LEP TEACHING METHODS

> EXPLORING THE POSSIBILITIES
> BUILDING THE NEXT GENERATION OF LEP
> EDUCATIONAL LEADERS

"Educators remind us that what counts in a classroom is not what the teacher teaches; it's what the learner learns."

—Alfie Kohn

REFRAMING EDUCATION THROUGH LEP TEACHING METHODS AND EXPLORING THE POSSIBILITIES

Reframing the way students are taught is an essential part of educational reform, and LEP teaching methods offer a new teaching initiative to affect that change. Reframing is having the insight to interpret occurrences and situations in divergent ways. It is also having the ability to choose the interpretation, solution, and perspective that is optimal for the required outcome. The need for educators to reframe teacher preparation and teaching methods from the traditional model, which is content absorption and memorization memory based, to an inclusive personal model such as the LEP teaching method, cannot be overstated. LEP is so effective because it offers unique, personalized learning and gives students the opportunity to connect to the information they are learning personally, thus moving the information from content absorption to content connection along with tools, techniques, and the environment necessary for learning and retaining information learned long-term.

LEP teaching methods, through inquisitive reflection, provide entry points into fundamentally reconceptualizing the meaning of quality learning and long-term memory retention. Reframing the methods and content taught, that is, the means and meaning of teaching, provides educators with opportunities to sharpen their own teaching skills and develop better learning and memory retention skills in their students. This change in approach of how the content is presented and the focus on inclusion of student sharing and interactions as related to concepts being learned necessitate student involvement in the course and increase student engagement, providing a robust environment of learning where individual memories shared become collective knowledge used for learning purposes.

To meet the demands of the LEP teaching methods, as with any other teaching method, is hard work. Educators are busy and have multiple demands in their personal and academic life, solving numerous logistic issues and developing themselves to establish new definitions of teaching and learning. However, stimulating students must be included in this equation. In short, students must be engaged to be retained. Ways to include LEP's inquisitive reflection as a tool for learning and move information being learned from content absorption to personal content connection among the range of diversified students in the classroom and online must be incorporated for students to be interested, learn in new ways, see the relevance of what they are learning, and retain the information in long-term memory.

When fully implemented, LEP teaching methods provide essential changes in traditional approaches to learning and teaching practices to engage, retain students, and increase the memory retention of the material learned. Teaching methods traditionally focus on procedures and processes where the memorization of new information has the lead role, without considering the personal contexts of individual students, such as memories of lived experiences as learning tools. This lack of consideration can weaken the effectiveness of the educator as teacher and increases the number of disenfranchised students. Disenfranchised students will not be retained for long.

The challenge is not only in capturing relationships with students and providing new information but creating new relationships out of old paradigms. Educators may still teach with traditional paradigms as these frameworks have been tried, tested, and proven effective. All educators have used various educational models that withstood the test of time but infusing LEP into the course work and allowing students to travel the unchartered territory of their lived experiences in the classroom and using these experiences to refine and develop greater clarity of the material being learned and retain that information long-term exceed traditional methods of learning.

LEP teaching methods do not eschew traditional methods but expand the limits in which students learn to include a partnership strategy of shared responsibility for student learning. Just as the student must be open to personal sharing through reflection to learn, the educator must be the role model and facilitator of the lived experience for the students and must share their own personal examples, to set the tone and provide the optimal environment for LEP learning to take place. If applied correctly, the LEP teaching methods provide an immense learning experience that triggers the expansion and understanding of topics studied, and increases student engagement, and productivity.

LEP teaching methods, through inquisitive reflection, provide a means of reframing learning in substantial and important ways. LEP is demographically friendly, where age, culture, education, and social or economic status are all equal learning tools. The understanding of concepts is filtered through cognitive processing, which is unique to each individual, increasing comprehension of material learned and memory retention within each student in a uniquely personal way. The information being learned is seen through a personal perspective and understood through a personal understanding. Understood from a personal viewpoint, the information is assimilated with prior memories and expanded to include the new information, thus forming a stronger bond in comprehension and memory.

LEP teaching and learning enables irreversible, profound change for the better—in information seeking, information connection, and student engagement and memory retention. The LEP teaching method addresses and explores core values, world views, beliefs, perspectives, personal patterns, existing knowledge, frameworks, and so on; in other words, it is interested in the lived experience of the students and their "meaning schemas" that the students use for thinking, perceiving, and imagining. These schemas through LEP's inquisitive inquiry are easily applied to memory when learning new content to transform learning from just "content absorption" and trigger existing memories to create "content connection," which leads to a personal association with the information being learned, and vastly assists with long-term retention. The visual memory hacks conclude the learning exercises as they provide a means to retrieve information from memory when needed.

The LEP teaching method is the vehicle of change within the current higher education system that improves student engagement, in-class retention, and learning and course outcomes and increases the memory retention of learned material.

Observable data indicated an increase in student engagement and attendance, evaluations and assessments, and increased learning outcomes when teaching with the LEP methods. Reframing education through LEP teaching methods offers hope opportunities and possibilities for all educators to enhance their teaching quality and foster engagement on all levels of student performance—from those deemed academically at risk to those designated as honor students.

BUILDING THE NEXT GENERATION OF LEP EDUCATIONAL LEADERS

LEP teaching methods offer educators an opportunity to become a positive force for educational change, and increase student learning, engagement, and in-school retention. The qualities of an LEP educational leader mirror the qualities of other educational leaders using other methods, with a slight deviation. The inclusion of inquisitive reflection and moving the student from content absorption to content connection is a fresh approach that makes material relevant to students, offers real-life applications, enhances students' creativity and critical thinking skills, and increases understanding, learning outcomes, and memory retention because the student is infused with an authentic and highly personal learning experience.

In this scenario, LEP educators are more than just people who helps students acquire knowledge, but are active participants guiding their students' personal learning. LEP educators work tirelessly to create challenging, trusting, and nurturing environments for their students in which to learn. Educators are not just subject matter experts who exhibit expertise in the subjects they are teaching, but are inspirational leaders who must inspire, arouse, and enthuse a diversified range of students and engage them in the material presented.

Many factors play a role in the effectiveness and performance of educators. Academic and course credentials, knowledge, experience, critical thinking, and other aspects of intelligence, along with good communication and listening skills, are essential to be effective as an educator. Friendliness and congeniality in a supportive and collaborative environment, where the educator is approachable, and sharing personal, but not private, information with the class relative to the topic under study strengthen engagement and interaction. This more relaxed classroom setting is also effective in putting students at ease and will lead to better communication, and ultimately a better leaning environment with increased learning outcomes, and memory retention of the information learned.

Often the difference between an effective teacher and a high-performing teacher is the mindset to achieve high learning, to think out of the box, and to be creative. In an age of scripted lessons and administrative accountability, creative thinking is taking a back seat. However, Pink (2005) notes that creative thinking is increasingly necessary in today's world. Sanders and Rivers (1996) concluded that the most important factor affecting student learning is the teacher; thus, it only makes sense to utilize LEP teaching methods, a creative teaching strategy with highly effective results, to enhance teaching practices of educators and move from effective to high-performing teaching practices.

Effective LEP educators improve their teaching through expanding the power of students' memories to be used as learning tools in the classroom. LEP educators expand their students' thoughts and understanding and instill the power of reflective practice in their learning. The practice of LEP's inquisitive reflection in the classroom can take an effective teacher to high performance and uncover hidden treasures, possibilities, and tools that can be used to infuse new life in old course work, learning, and teaching approaches.

LEP educators are skilled at providing opportunities for students to take on both ownership and leadership roles in their very personal learning, which vastly increases students' interest, engagement and memory retention of material learned. LEP educators have the ability to turn their personal curiosities and creativity into valuable teaching techniques, and weave in personal interests, and their lived experience, to student learning and problem solving. For example, a math teacher with an interest in history can integrate history into math word problems and math vignettes, and use these personal examples to explain and solve the problem.

LEP educators are highly inclusive, having complete regard for the progress and personal development of each student. LEP educators must also be self-aware, have an understanding of themselves, and have the confidence to use LEP's inquisitive reflection freely to tap into their own memories and memories of their students to assist in the understanding and memory retention of the content. Having a clear vision of how LEP will be applied in the classroom and ways to promote fruitful opportunities for learning must be planned out well in advance.

LEP educators must show confidence in the LEP inquisitive reflection techniques to trigger the students to follow the educators' lead. By speaking positively of the immense results that can be attained by using the LEP learning and memory process, students will acquire a belief in it as well and use it to their full advantage. LEP educators' should have consistent high expectations and demonstrate how LEP is an advantage to students' learning achievements and how their past lived experience is a valuable learning tool. Continuously communicating with students is of vital importance. Talk to your students; a good educational leader cannot lead without interaction from their followers. Interact with your students as much as possible and always be the example, and optimal learning and significant increases in course and learning outcomes will occur.

High-performing educators know that they must reach students in diverse ways. LEP is the power that allows high-performing teaching to reach all students. LEP teaching methods allow for the magic of learning to be engaging, fun, and memorable with new learning curves at every opportunity as students are influenced and affected in their own unique way and are able to process new material through their personal perception and prior frameworks of existing information.

LEP educators must focus relentlessly and continually on improving teaching and learning through LEP. The LEP educator must be robust and rigorous in terms of self-evaluation and data analysis, with clear strategies for improvement. Students are hungry to learn, but learning must be relevant to them if they are to be engaged and retained. Thus, the LEP educator must be skilled in turning around challenges, obstacles, and mind blocks and work relentlessly on behalf of students to motivate and inspire them to use LEP to meet their learning outcomes.

High-performing LEP educators create a positive change in the educational system, in their students, and in themselves. By showing a passion for the material being taught and creatively using LEP's inquisitive reflection in their course work LEP educators will inspire their students to want to learn more, and show them the relevancy of the material to their lives, which results in increased student engagement, retention, and learning outcomes. Set high expectations, as it greatly affects achievement; be creative, motivated, and sustained by the knowledge that "teaching is a profession that makes all other professions possible."

CHAPTER TEN

LEP Class Supplements and Resources

> Mind Preparation
> Student Worksheets and Activities
> Educator Preparation List

Chapter 10 includes student worksheets, activities, the LEP course preparation checklist, and simple instructions for creative visualization and mental imaginary guidance that students may follow when preparing to work with memories through inquisitive reflection. All worksheets and activities were deliberately kept basic to allow for modifications and adjustments by educators. Educators are encouraged to customize each sheet to a specific course or lesson plan or create their own LEP worksheets and activities to suit the educator or student needs.

For students who *cannot* connect to concepts through past memories, LEP imagination worksheets should be used to learn, remember, and retrieve information. Instead of utilizing inquisitive reflection to connect a topic to experiences (memories), these students will use their **imagination** and academic **concept definition** and description to move from content absorption **connect** to the new information in a personal way. All worksheets can be modified to replace the word "memories" with the world "imagination" to include concept imagination scenarios. (See the example in Activity 13.)

MIND PREPARATION

Before working with inquisitive reflection, it is recommended to take part in rhythmic breathing to settle, clear, and refocus the mind to the subject matter at hand. Rhythmic breathing balances the body and clears the mind, which assists in information flow. There are many variations of breathing techniques, but generally breathing in for eight counts, holding for eight counts, and releasing for eight counts quiets the mind. (Each set of eight should be repeated three to five times).

The students must be mentally prepared to inquisitively reflect and search for memories to connect to concepts being learned and have a quiet place to do so. It is *not* uncommon for strong emotions to surface as the mind explores memories relative to the concepts studied and for various interpretations and meanings to result from the investigative inquiry. The optimal memory of the experience that is the most similar to the true academic interpretation of the concept and which expands understanding and personal application would yield the best connection, and is the ideal building block to expand concept definition and build memory hacks for easy retrieval of information later.

At first, having difficulty concentrating may occur, but students are to be made aware that often this is expected and that with practice this process will become innate. Should thoughts stray, students are to redirect their focus to the topic at hand. It is important to note that the student is not just exploring the moments in their mind looking to connect their experience to concepts learned, but reliving the moment in that time, space, and place, which allows for the possibility for students to see concepts in new light, and are able to apply concept meanings in many creative ways. Connecting the experience relative to the concept under study manifests in a much deeper and richer interpretation and understanding of the material and greatly assists in long-term memory retention.

Activity 1

CREATIVE VISUALIZATION AND IMAGERY

The role of silence and a quiet place: Clearing the mind preparation

Any stressors and preoccupations can negatively impact content absorption, content connection, and memory retention. Before engaging in learning, students should clear their mind of all distraction and discord and prepare themselves mentally to receive new information. They should not only focus on what they are learning but also visualize how this information can be useful to them.

Student activity:

- **Review** the assignment and identify the content you wish to retain

- **Write** down the book definition of the key concepts

- **Write** down your understanding of the concept(s) based on the book interpretation

- Using **inquisitive reflection** visualize the content as you understand it and try to remember a scenario in your life where the concept was in operation. If you cannot remember a time where this concept operated in your life imagine what would it be like if it did appear, Asking questions in the inquisitive reflection state in vital to content connections.

    How does this concept relate to you, your life? What is the closest association you have in your memory that you can identify this concept with? Why did you, or what made you, think of this scenario as it related to the concept? Which trigger category are you using to connect with the concept? Why are you using this particular trigger category?

- Continue to use either existing memories or the imagination to **visualize** the concept and how you see it applied in your life. See the concept working in your life. How is it operating? How is it beneficial? How can you use it to your advantage? If it is not working, why not? Visualize how you wish to see this information used in your life. Visualize why it is important for you to know more about it. Visualize retaining this information in your long-term memory. Visualize and see the memory hack you will use to recall this information later.

    It is important to not only visualize the concept working in your life but also feel what it feels like with all the emotions associated with it. Imagine that you are a higher facet of your own consciousness as you search for a memory that relates to the concept under study. By simple **intent,** *your desire to do it, you can find and merge with any appropriate memory to uncover vast meaning and knowledge you may already possess relative to the concept and frame it for your optimal understanding. If you cannot connect to an experience, use your imagination— ask questions; based on what you know, what do you imagine the concept to be? Using the information in the textbooks, how do you imagine the concept working in your life? Students should imagine the concept operating in their life through various trigger categories, as it greatly expands concept application choices.*

- **Record visualizations**: After visualization, write down the lived experiences that surfaced that reflects or relates to the concept. If you cannot connect the concept to your experience, use information gathered from imagination. Write down **how** and **why** it relates to the concept. **Write** down the **trigger** that corresponds to the concept and the selected memory hack that will be used to retrieve the memory of the information when needed and explain why you are using it.

- **Visualize the memory hack:** Take your time, reflect, contemplate, and record all associated factors and emotions as related to the concept(s) under study for a deeper understanding and application of the concept's relevance to your life. Recording information is very important as the very act of writing reinforces information in the human long-term memory.

- After you have made and recorded the connection between content absorption (just understanding the content) to content connection (see the applicability and meaning in your life), and have a memory hack in place to retrieve the information when needed, spend a few extra minutes to further reinforce the memory by using **creative visualization to imagine** all the great benefits that you will have as a result of knowing this information. By utilizing creative visualization and expecting positive outcomes, learning becomes fun and memorable, as it allows students to see the future possibilities of the new knowledge and their personal applicability to their own life and/or the world at large.

Activity 2

LEP Inquisitive Reflection Activity

1. Quiet the mind but breathe naturally. (To quiet the mind LEP utilizes contemplation through meditation). Meditation trains the mind the way physical fitness trains the body. The intention is to silence all thoughts by ignoring everything that does not have to do with exploration of the connection of the concept to the student's existing frame of understanding (lived experience). Meditation should be 15 - 30 minutes per concept. If the mind wanders it must be brought back to the concept. Students should relax and visualize lived experiences that may be connected to concepts as visualization will keep the students on point and interrupt the assault of thoughts that randomly affect focus. All trigger categories should be considered before final selection to use as a tool to relate to the concept/s and link to memories of lived experiences for framing understanding and application of the concept.

2. In meditative mode, reflectively and objectively explore your memories to link them with concepts being learned. Reflect by connecting personal philosophies, lived experiences, and your current knowledge of the concept. Do not rush the process, but investigatively reflect. Have I seen this before? Have I experienced something similar? What existing framework or understanding do I already have about this concept? How can I connect this concept to my lived experience so that I can understand it better, and see how this information is relevant in my life? The inquisitive reflection phase examines situations, events, feelings, emotions, personal knowledge, and existing information as it pertains to content learned and offers opportunities to use critical thinking to find old patterns and entertain new ways of thinking and review past decisions, actions or situations as it relates to the concept being learned. Probing and questioning during reflection are critical and are strongly encouraged.

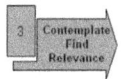

3. Once a memory trigger category is selected, through inquisitive reflection and find relevance in this information. Why was this memory selected over others to connect to the concept? Why is this information important to you? How can you use it in the future? Relevant information means that something is interesting, and useful to current learning. Relevant and meaningful connections activate the learning process. Students are encouraged to gauge the relevance of the material they are learning, as this helps students see how the content fits into their current framework, and future point of reference. Students should not rush this process but immerse themselves in the efforts to see how this information can serve them in their existing personal framework, and in the future. Use your imagination!

4. Creating new meaning from established forms of reference and frameworks: After contemplation organize thoughts and ideas that immersed from existing memories, and memory triggers, so that new or different learning from existing information as it relates to the content under study is facilitated. New meaning comes from the integration of textbook understanding of the concept and personal LEP memories which expand understanding of the concept and shows its various applications for a clearer interpretation which assists in expansion of knowledge and students' growth. By assigning new meaning and assimilating information from triggered information new learning to existing schemas will expand knowledge and understanding of topic.

5. Use information from memory trigger to create a memory hack to retrieve it. Relevant, meaningful learning engages students emotionally and connects with their existing knowledge which assists in building neural connections and long-term memory storage: Create a mental memory of the lived experience and how it related to the concept and write down the information. Review the information at various intervals, as repetition and visualizations are effective forms of learning. Once the information is assimilated and rooted in memory, choose a personal trigger that will be solely connected to the concept to remember the information. The trigger must be closely related to the concept, and all senses, personality traits, humor or any other LEP experience can be used as a trigger to recall the needed information. Be in the moment when encoding personal trigger to memory, this will set the stage to evoke the trigger when the information is needed. The trigger reminds the brain where the information is stored thereby recall is easier.

Activity 3

QUICK INQUISITIVE REFLECTION—PRACTICE SHEET

Let your curiosity about yourself generate answers for your content. This is an open-ended at-a-glance exercise outlining a quick process of investigative reflection, where you will actively investigate, inquire, question, examine, and assess your memories to connect them to the content learned. Practice inquisitive reflection by following the quick exercise when searching your memories to assist you in new learning. The more you practice, the more you will be able to probe deeper and establish various connections to the new information, which will greatly assist in understanding and long-term retention of material. (If you cannot connect to an experience relative to the concept learned, use your imagination).

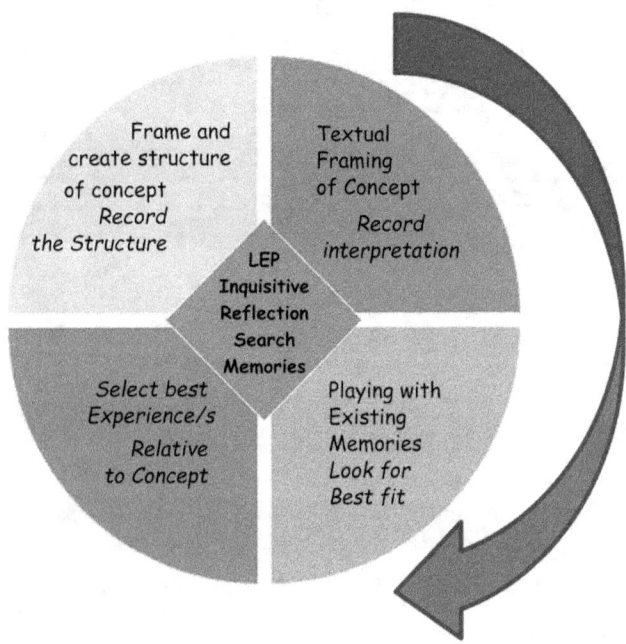

Activity 4
CONTENT ABSORPTION TO CONTENT CONNECTION

Practicing with Content Absorption to Content Connections Worksheets

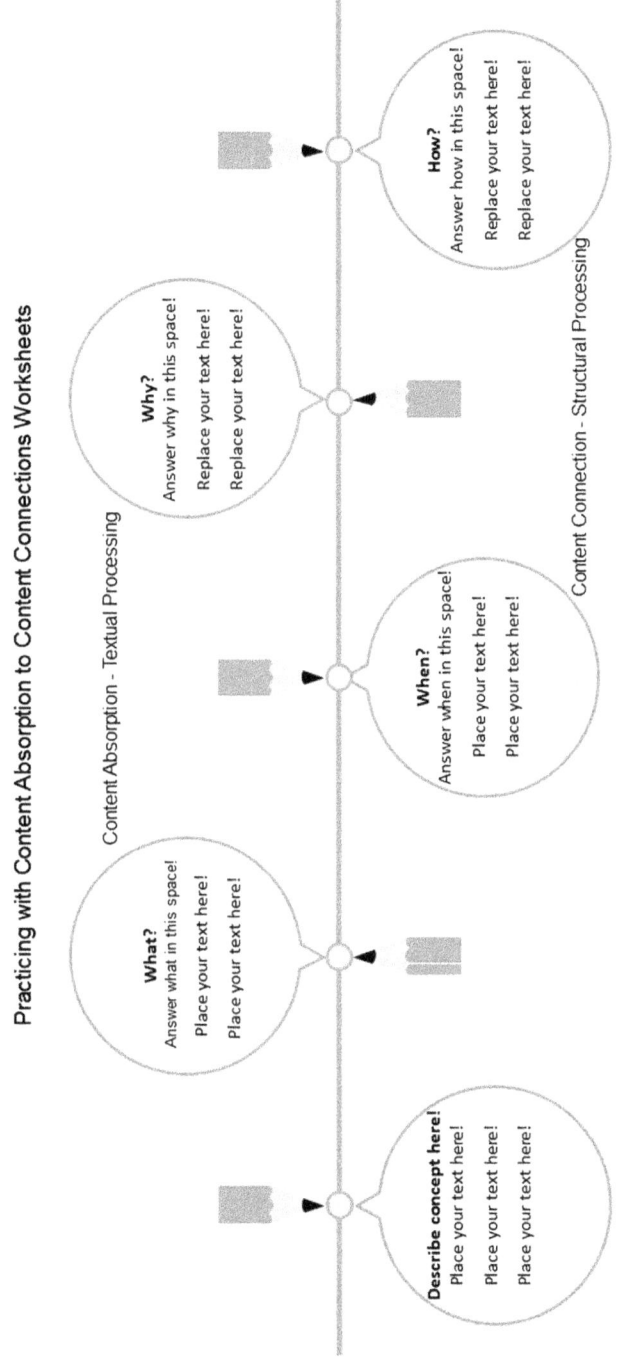

Describe your concept here in a well rounded summary using both your textual and structural interpretations from above:

CHAPTER TEN LEP CLASS SUPPLEMENTS AND RESOURCES

Activity 5

LEP Textual and Structural Mapping Practice Sheet

CONCEPT:

LEP Textual and Structural Mapping	
TEXTUAL	**STRUCTURAL**
Textual Description	Essence, Core, Application
• Read about the concept multiple times and take notes • Annotate your concept description with every read through and add more details • Add image, doodle, rough sketch your thoughts etc. • Summarize the textbook definition and your understanding of the concept in the textual box below.	• Identify and describe general ideas, and the essence of the concept and how you think it may fit in your world. (Thoughts should center on what is at the core of the concept, and personal meaning that can be drawn). • Using inquisitive reflection search your memories for experiences, or moments in your life that relate to the concept. (Each reflection selected must relate somehow to the concept and offer new expansion of understanding and personal application of the concept). • It is important to carefully review existing memories and look for the one association that fits best. Structural interpretations add to textual knowledge to expand definition/s and understanding of the concept and how the concept relates to the student personally, as it structures textual definitions. • Summarize the structural applications in the structural box below.

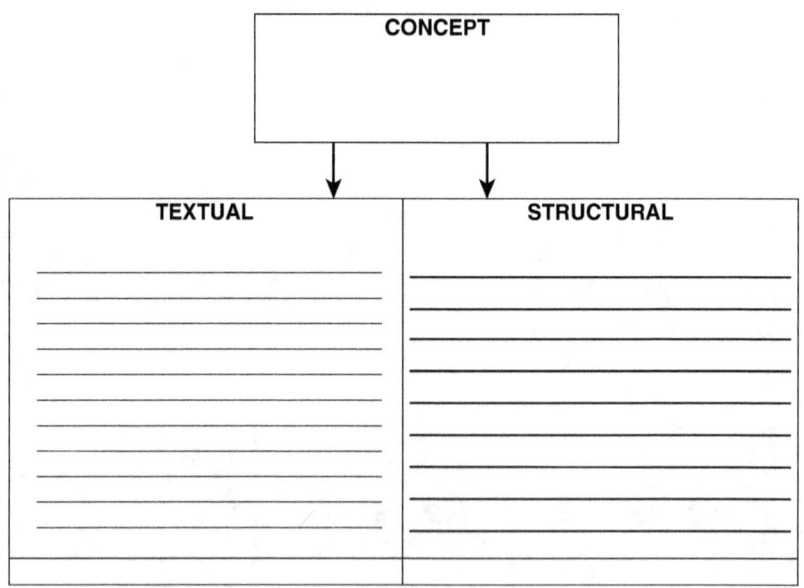

Activity 6

UNDERSTANDING THE LEP FRAMING PROCESS

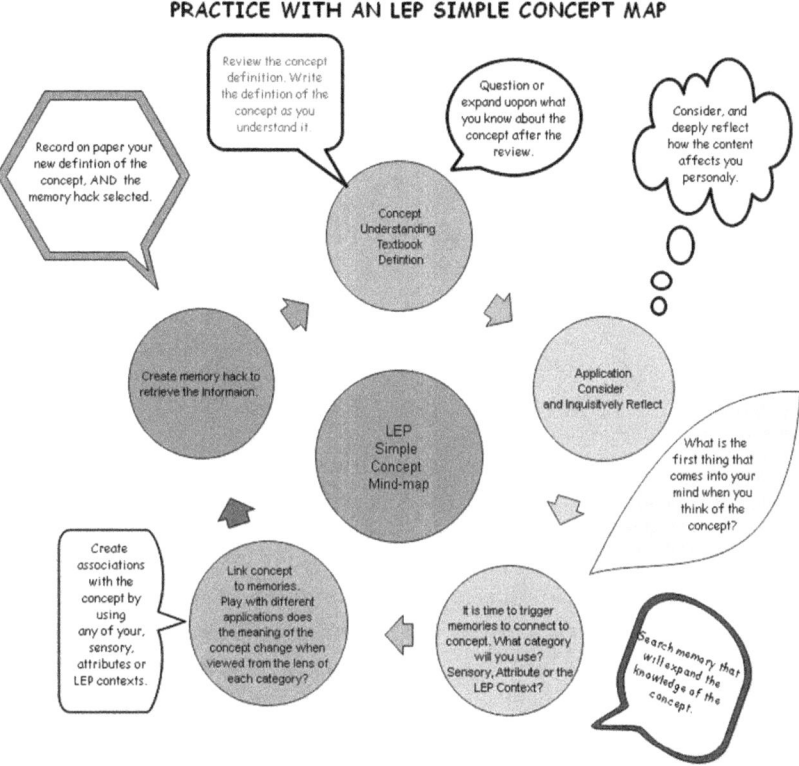

The educator should assist students in understanding the process of framing to enable them to form generalizations that link the concept with their memories in a way that expands their knowledge on the topic and where the information makes sense. Very often, using an example to frame the concept for the student in advance assists in faster connections to their lived experience memories and expanded understanding and application(s) of the concept.

Framing is a feature of the human brain's structural design mechanism. The human mind reacts to the context in which something is embedded and tries to find patterns or existing blueprints to create meaning. To frame a concept through LEP's inquisitive inquiry, students search their memories for an event or a situation that most closely resembles the concept definition under study. Once a lived experience is identified, the students focus on the relationships between their current understanding of the concept and the main ideas and details of their lived experience. There is an unfolding of patterns and structures from the exploration of the lived experiences as they are related to new concepts as the framing process begins, which is followed by meaning. (If an experience cannot be identified, students should use their imagination to create an appropriate connection that fits the true definition of concept).

Understanding the Four Steps of LEP Framing

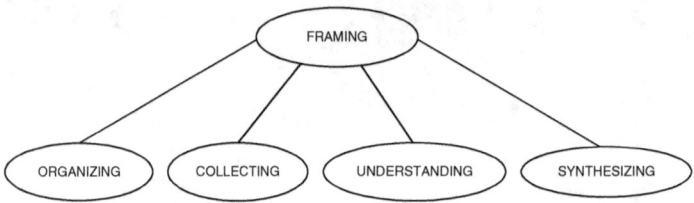

1. **Framing:** Frame your thoughts, memories, and ideas using LEP inquisitive reflection. Approach framing as an open-ended process with existing information reframed regularly to accommodate and assimilate new information.

2. **Framing organizes and collects information:** Think about what you already know about the concept and write it down. How and in what capacity does the lived experience relate to the concept? Describe the experience. What were the significant factors? Why did you think of this particular experience to frame the understanding of this concept? Record the factors that relate to the lived experience and use those experiences and factors to frame the concept to give it personal meaning (structure).

3. **Framing for understanding:** Framing sets the context for understanding concepts. Framing exists to help students make sense of incoming information and influences how the concept is interpreted, and the meaning it is assigned.

4. **Framing for synthesizing:** Synthesis is not just a summary of your concepts but includes deep inquisitive reflections that produce deep insights. Thus, ensure that your framing activity includes more than just a summary, which in essence is just basic structure of the concepts description, but also includes well-thought-out understanding and interpretation of the concept and its connection and application to your life.

Activity 7

CONCEPT FRAMING WORKSHEET

To practice framing concepts, you can create your own template by placing any concept in the center of a sheet of paper and fill in the appropriate boxes as seen in the concept framing worksheet example. The diagram is split in visual ways, which includes textbook definition of the concept, facts that include knowledge you may already possess, and information from lecture notes and so on relative to the concept. The worksheet also includes sections relative to the application of the concept and spaces to record triggered memories of your experiences, or the ways in which you can apply the concept in your life or the world at large. How does the concept as seen through your experience influence or assist you or the world at large?

Probe deeper into your memories and based on the textbook definition, and the factual knowledge you already know about the concept, connect with your memories to give your concept a structural frame. Use one or more trigger categories to search for memories, sensory triggers, LEP attributes, or the LEP contexts, to expand and frame your understanding and personal application of the concept(s) and record the information in the appropriate boxes. (You may use any memory trigger category, or a combination of memory trigger categories, and record the information in the appropriate box).

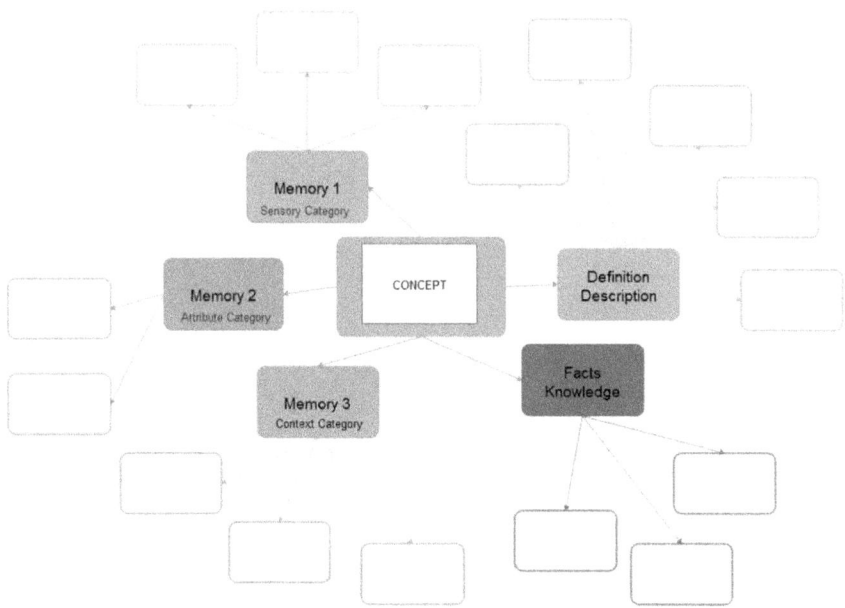

Student Activity 8a

FRAMING WITH SENSORY MEMORY TRIGGERS

Explain the concept in the first box by using information from your textbook, lecture notes, or any educational resource. Use sight, smell, feel, sound, taste, or touch or a combination of senses to trigger memories that relate to the concept. Record the memories in the appropriate boxes. (Since framing through the senses can be confusing at first, see activity 8a for a completed worksheet to serve as a visual example.)

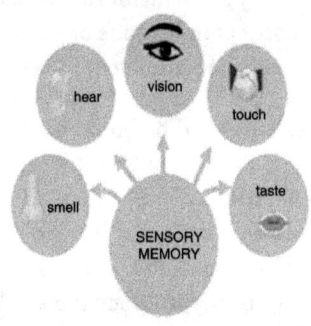

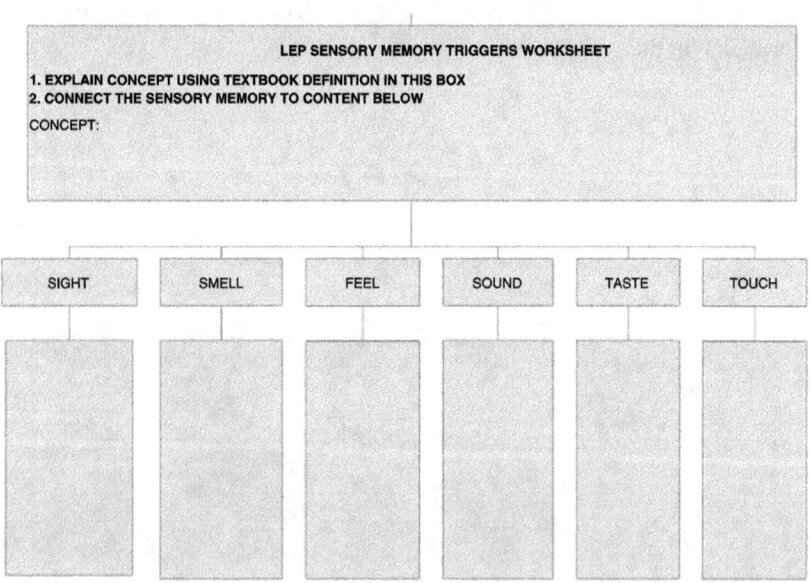

Activity 8b

VISUAL EXAMPLE OF CREATING SENSORY TRIGGERS AND HACKS

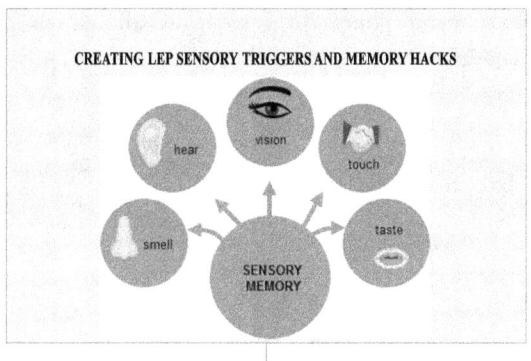

EXPLAIN CONCEPTS USING TEXTBOOK DEFINITION IN THIS BOX AND CONNECT THE SENSORY MEMORY TO CONCEPT BELOW

Concept Example: Ego, the "I" of any person. The ego is a person's sense of self esteem or self importance when dealing with reality, and often manifests in self illusion. The ego recognizes that being selfish is not always good for the person, but takes into consideration what others will think. According to the Freudian model of the psyche the ego is the organized, realistic part that negotiates between the id and the superego.

Choose one or more "sense" to apply the concept (EGO) in your life and complete the box/es below.

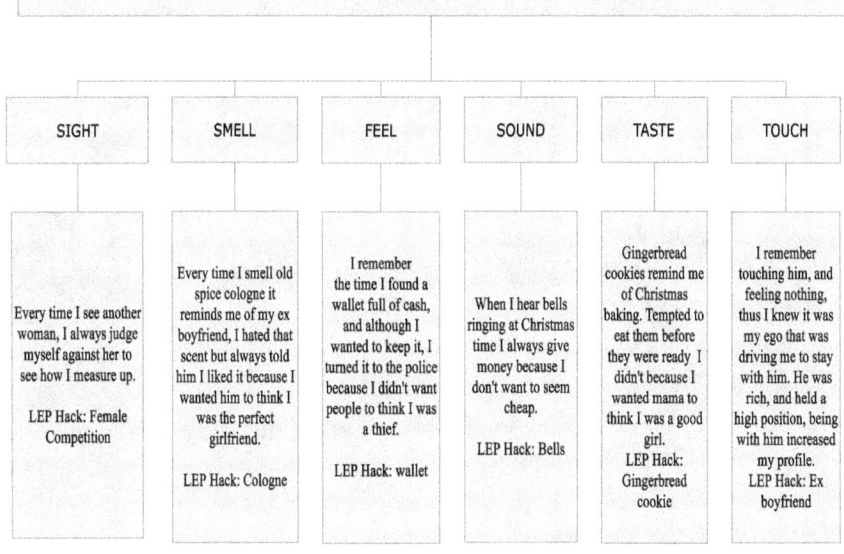

CHAPTER TEN LEP CLASS SUPPLEMENTS AND RESOURCES

Activity 9

OVERVIEW OF LEP MEMORY TRIGGER CATEGORIES

Students should use the below LEP memory trigger categories at-a-glance overview for a quick reference when trying to connect concepts to lived experiences for concept expansion and application, as it outlines all three categories of sensory, LEP attributes, and LEP contexts in detail.

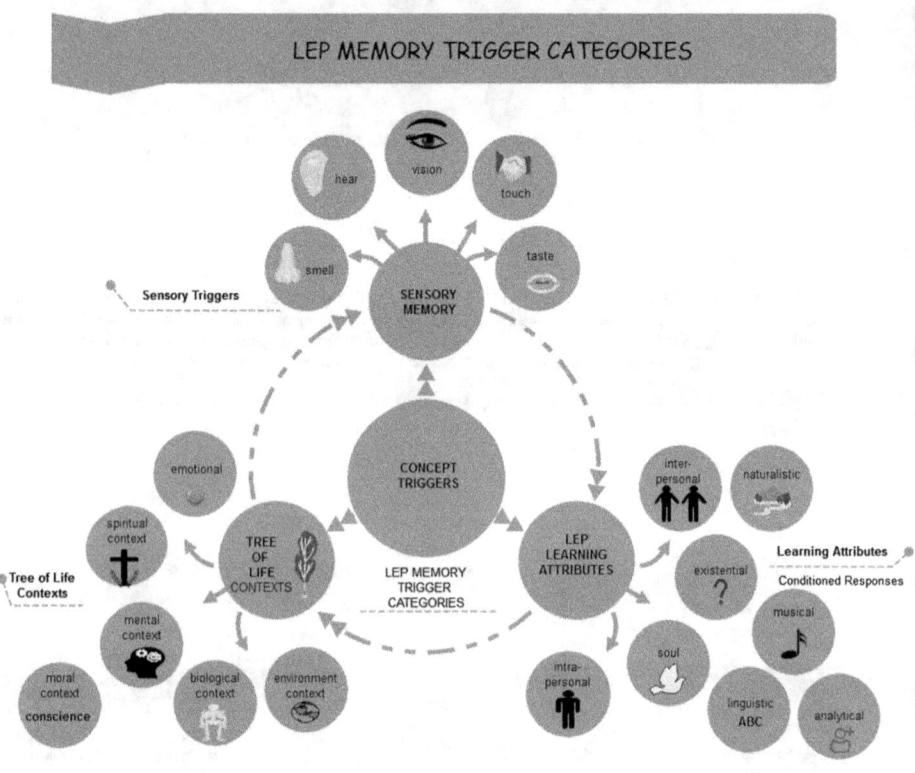

Student Activity 10

LEP Trigger Attribute Practice Worksheet

Start at the center. Define the concept using your notes, or textbook, then let your eyes move over each image to connect to the attribute of the image that resonates with you the most. Read the description to find the best fit in which to view the concept. When your mind triggers a memory that relates best to the concept record the memory that was triggered in the box, and its association to the concept. If desired, to reinforce the trigger, sketch it or insert an image in the last box. (If a memory does not surface use your IMAGINATION to connect to concept).

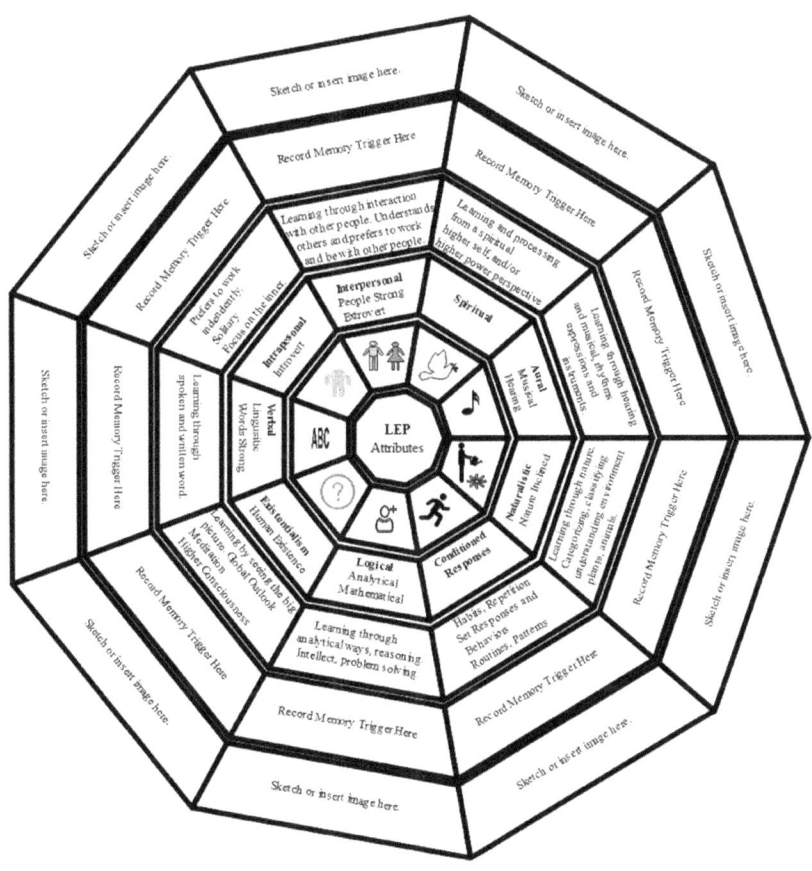

Activity 11

LEP Context Tree Visual Activity for Inquistive Reflection

Play with memory triggers using the LEP context tree. Review each trigger category. Which trigger will you use to frame the concept? As your eyes move over the words, how does the concept resonate with you? Which category of emotional, physical, mental, spiritual/universal, or environmental will you use as your memory trigger to connect to the concept?

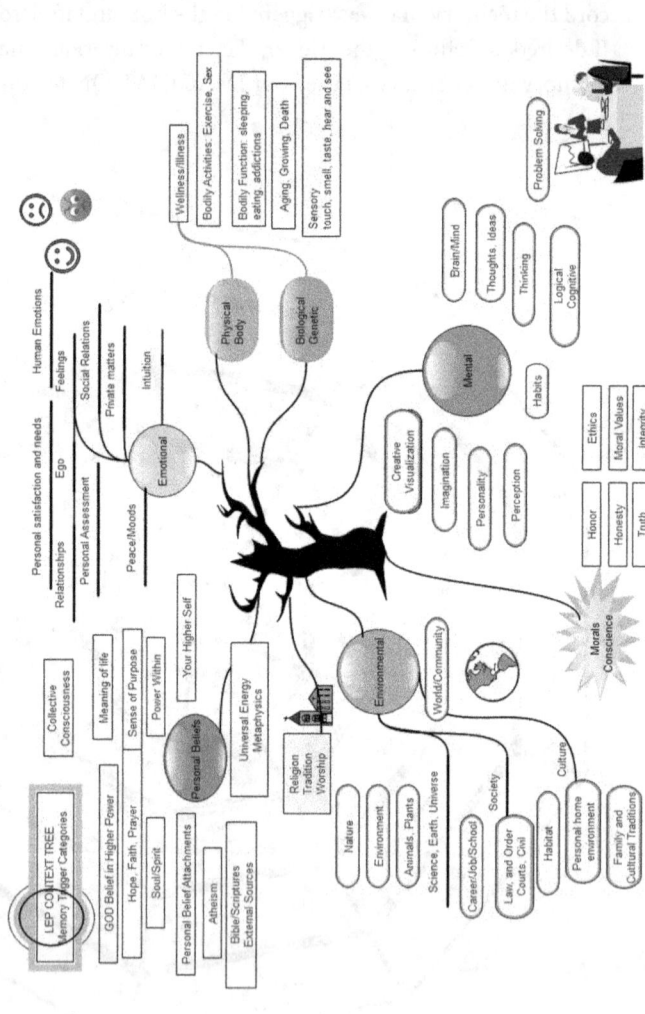

144 LIVED EXPERIENCE PHENOMENON LEP BOOK 2

Activity 12

CREATE MEMORY HACK

CONCEPT DEFINITION AND APPLICATION:

Practice creating memory hacks by using your imagination and creative visualization! Use the diagram below for a refresher of each memory trigger category; sensory memory, LEP attributes, and LEP context to create your memory hacks.

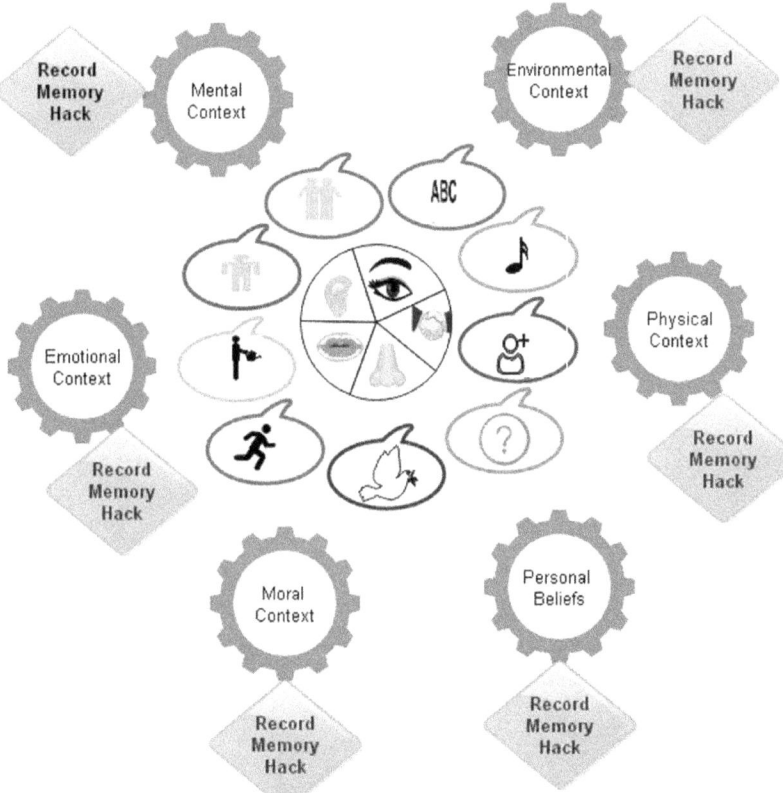

Activity 13

USING IMAGINATION INSTEAD OF MEMORIES

If memories relative to understanding the concepts are not immediately available, review the concept definition and use your imagination to link to and expand concept definition. In what way can this concept be applied in real life? Be creative; as long as the imagined scenario is in line with the concepts' true definition, it is of no consequence whether the scenario is real or imagined. Practice LEP inquisitive reflection through your imagination by filling in the boxes as it applies with the concept(s) information you are learning.

Using Imagination to Connect to Concepts

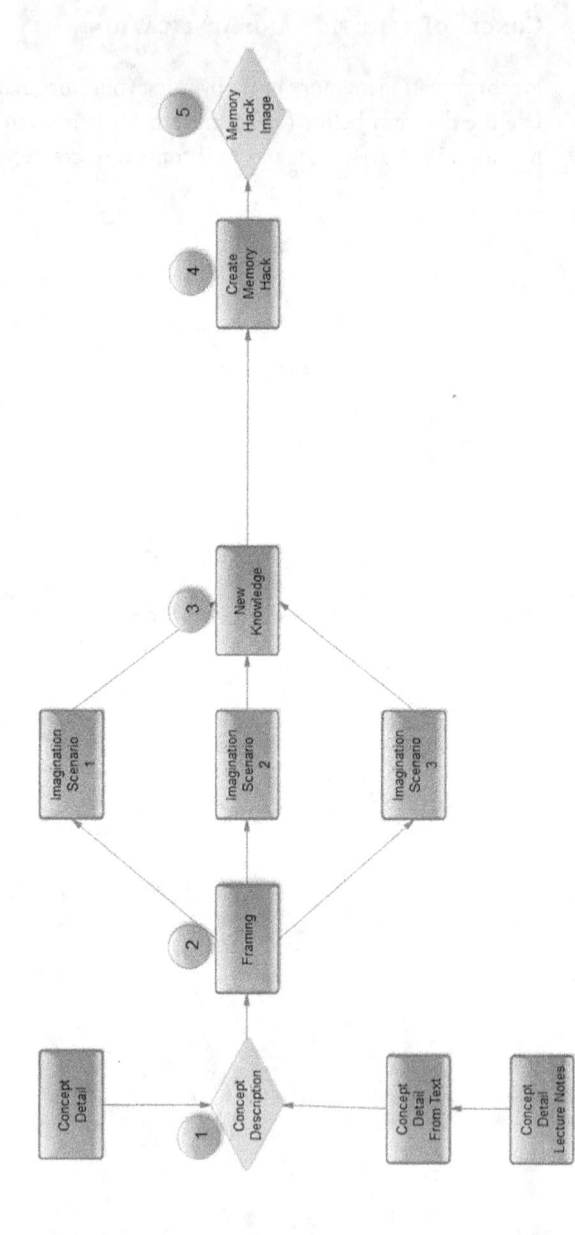

Activity 14

CHRONOLOGICAL PATTERN OF ORGANIZATION

Organization of ideas to create a memory hack is a very important step in the memory retrieval process. You can record information to create a memory hack using sensory information, innate attributes, or context triggers in a chronological process by completing the boxes below.

LEP Chronological Design Pattern
(Timeline or use Before or After)

Concept Application
Choose a trigger category to explain the concept using the chronological design pattern to organize your information, and create a memory hack for memory retrieval of information.

Sensory Triggers	Innate Attribute Triggers	LEP Context Triggers
Day, Month, Year, Season, Holiday, Special Markers etc.	Day, Month, Year, Season, Holiday, Special Markers etc.	Day, Month, Year, Season, Holiday, Special Markers etc.
Text	Text	Text
Text	Text	Text
Text	Text	Text
Text	Text	Text
Sketch or insert an image of your memory hack in this space.	Sketch or insert an image of your memory hack in this space.	Sketch or insert an image of your memory hack in this space.

Concept Summary:

Activity 15

SEQUENCE PATTERN OF ORGANIZATION

LEP ORGANIZATIONAL SEQUENCE PATTERN
Organizing Information and Creating Memory Hacks

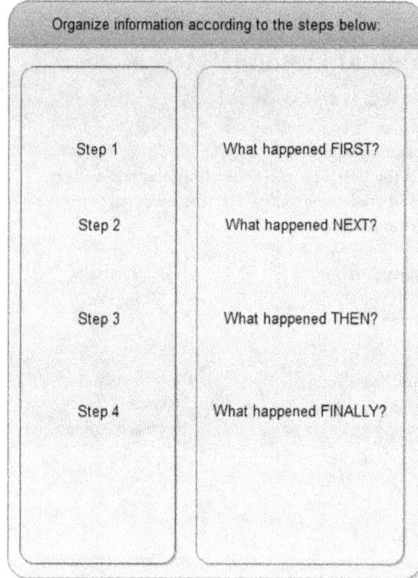
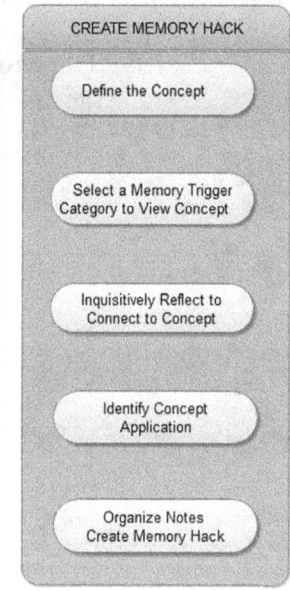

Notes should be taken at every step from gathering textbook knowledge, using lecture notes etc. and must include the memory triggers that were used to connect to the concept, personal applications, and memory hacks.

Activity 16

CAUSE-AND-EFFECT DESIGN PATTERN

CREATING PERSONAL MEMORY DESIGN: CAUSE-AND-EFFECT DESIGN MEMORY HACKS

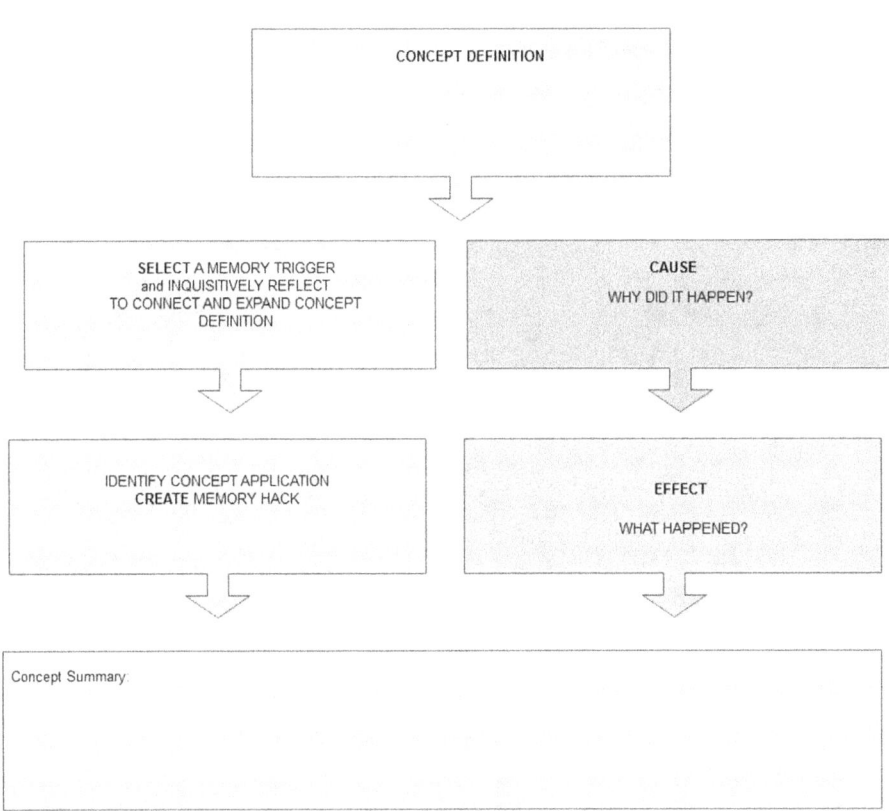

Activity 17

PROBLEM-AND-SOLUTION DESIGN PATTERN

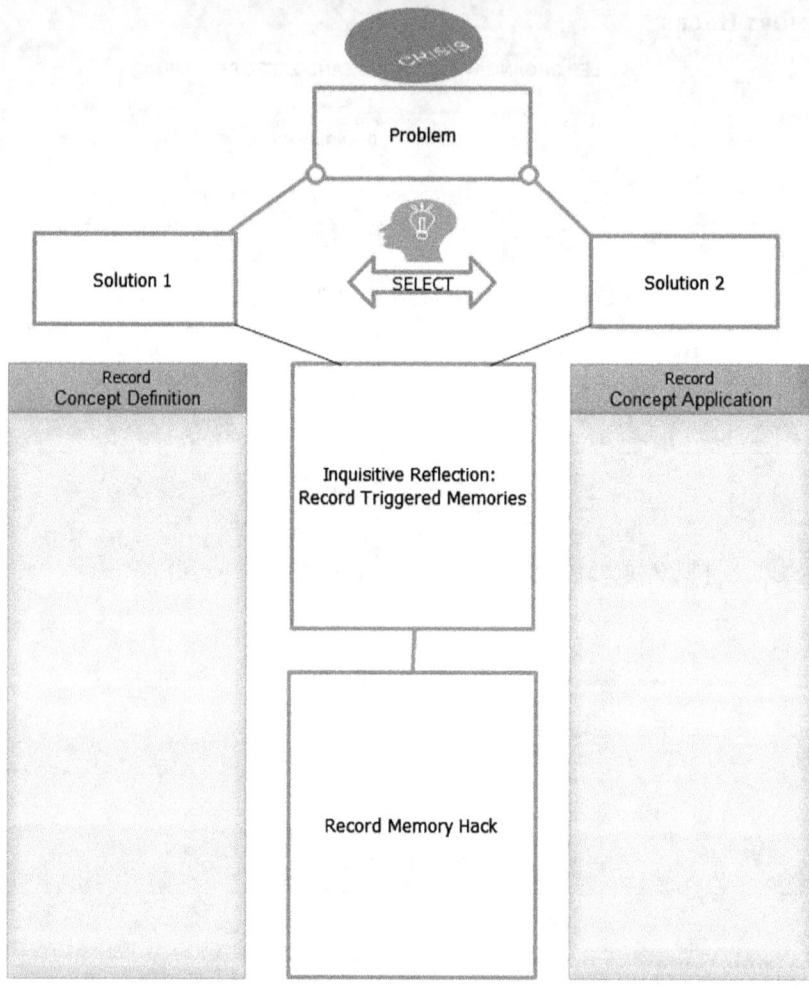

Activity 18

COMPARE-AND-CONTRAST DESIGN PATTERN

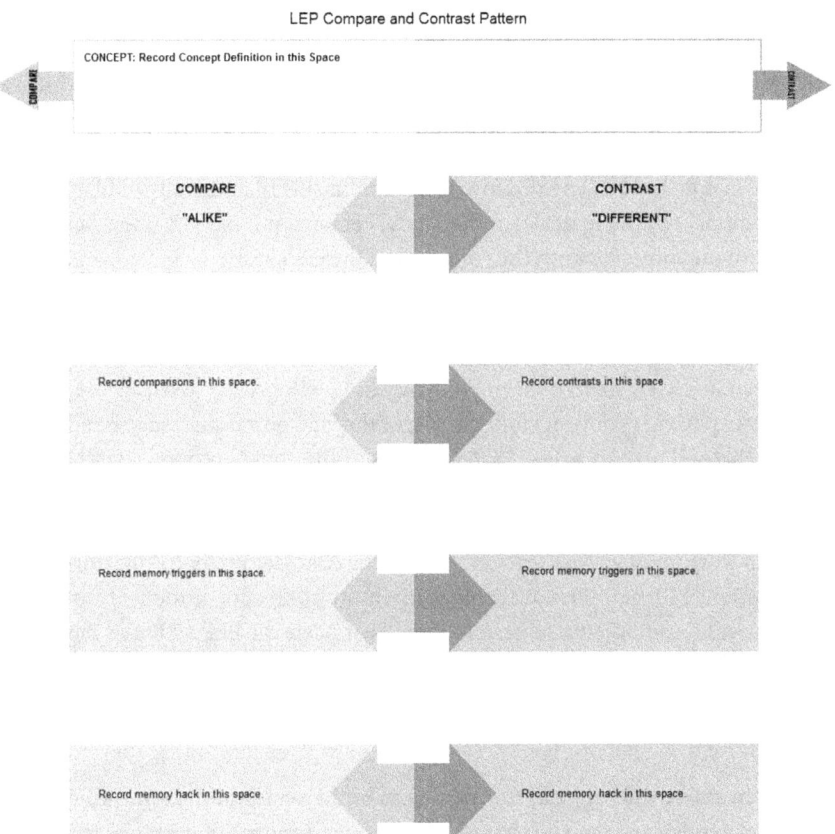

CHAPTER TEN LEP CLASS SUPPLEMENTS AND RESOURCES

LEP EDUCATOR PREPARATION CHECKLIST

Every educator must be aware of how the material being taught relates to the students' life. The material must be relevant and clear for student engagement so that they meet learning outcomes. When expecting student buy-in, educators must be prepared to share their personal experience. Educators should prepare at least two LEP examples and connect them to the concept or topic being learned to include within class discussion or post the information in the discussion board section of courses with online components. If students cannot connect to information, they *must* be encouraged to use their imagination; in this manner, all students will be able to connect to the material under study. Personal interaction is mandatory for successful outcomes by both the student and the educator.

Plan early and well. The importance of planning early for your course and having all the materials needed in class and available is crucial to optimal learning. Being organized and well structured in your planning will greatly assist in the smooth learning experiences of your students. Know the vital points that must be addressed in the class and plan to adjust LEP strategies as the course progresses, which may happen as a result of varied demographics of the class. This can be achieved through lecture formats, which include LEP examples, class discussions, written assignments or group work, or any other teaching format the educator prefers. Educators should have content LEP activities available early in the course for students to work and practice with. Additionally, educators should complete the LEP activities themselves so that they can experience the process they are asking their students to follow. The review of the worksheets will assist in modification that the educator may deem to be necessary to suit their specific discipline.

Create an active learning environment and build a classroom community where personal experiences can be shared to aid understanding of material presented. Educators should find ways to make students comfortable while sharing their LEPs as they relate to the content under discussion. An active and supportive learning environment promotes stronger connection to the material being learned, and an open and caring attitude and consistent behavior that encourages an environment of trust will assist in promoting a positive learning environment.

Educators take on the role of facilitator and monitor. The educator takes the lead, sets the examples, and directs the learning process. Educators must be prepared to facilitate, mediate, and monitor classroom discussions and group work, allowing room for expressions but must always be on hand to redirect the discussion to focal points of content to assist with allotted classroom time and topic. In the classroom setting, all students should have the opportunity to participate and explain why they chose a certain LEP to connect to the textbook concept, as this will reinforce memory and create an opportunity for students to share how they think this information is relevant and will serve them. The educator in the LEP educational space is more of a facilitator of knowledge rather than someone who just imparts knowledge.

REFERENCES

Barkley, J. R. (2008, September). *Making sense of place according to lived experience*. Champaign, IL: University of Illinois at Urbana-Champaign.

Bartlett, F. C. (1932). *Remembering: An experimental and social study*. New York, NY: Cambridge University Press.

Bough, K. (2015). *Our brains are wired for stories*. Retrieved from http://www.definingstory.com/Bough-Strackbein-Brain-Story.pdf

Brookfield, S. D. (2002). Using the lenses of critically reflective teaching in the community college classroom. *New Directions for Community Colleges, 118*, 31–38. doi.org/10.1002/cc.61

Costa, A., & Kallick, B. (2008). *Learning and leading with habits of mind: 16 Essential characteristics for success*. Alexandria, VA: ASCD Publishing.

Davis, S. E. (2007). Learning styles and memory. *Institute for Learning Styles Journal, 1*, 46–51.

Davis, S.E. (Fall, 2007). Institute for Learning Styles Journal, 1, p. 46–51.

Denzin, N. K. (1985). Emotion as lived experience. *Symbolic Interaction, 8*(2), 223–240.

Denzin, N. K. (1992). The many faces of emotionality. In Ellis & Flaherty (Eds.), *Investigating Subjectivity* (pp. 17–30), Newbury Park, CA: Sage.

Denzin, N. (2001). *Interpretive interactionism*. Thousand Oaks, CA: Sage.

DiClementi, J. D., & Handelsman, M. M. (2005). Empowering students: Class-generated course rules. *Teaching of Psychology, 32*, 18–21.

Dirkx, J. M. (2008). Engaging emotions in adult learning: A Jungian perspective on emotion and transformative learning. *New Directions for Continuing Education, 109*, 15–26. doi.org/10.1002/ace.204

Freiler, T. J. (2008). Learning through the body. *New Directions for Adult and Continuing Education, 119*, 37–47. doi: 10.1002/ace.304

Gardner, H. (1993). *Multiple intelligences: The theory in practice*. New York: Basic Books.

Gay, G. (2000). *Culturally responsive teaching: Theory, research, and practice*. New York: Teachers College Press.

Gendlin, E. T. (1996). *Focusing-oriented theory: A manual of the experiential method*. New York, NY: Guilford.

Gisquet-Verrier, P. Riccio, D. C. (2012). Memory reactivation effects independent of reconsolidation. *Learning and Memory, 19*, 401–409.

Goold, L., & Hummell, J. (1993). *Supporting the receptive communication of individuals with significant multiple disabilities: Selective use of touch to enhance comprehension*. North Rocks, Australia: The Royal New South Wales Institute for Deaf and Blind Children.

Harnish, R. J., O'Brien McElwee, R., Slattery, J. M., Frantz, S., Haney, M. R., Shore, C. M., & Penley, J. (2011). Creating the foundation for a warm classroom climate: Best practices in syllabus tone. *APS Observer, 24*, 23–27.

Harnish, R. J. & Bridges, R. K. (September, 2011). Effect of syllabus tone: Students' perceptions of instructor and course. *Social Psychology of Education: An International Journal, 14*(3), p. 319–330)

Hopper, C. (2015). *Practicing college learning strategies.* Boston, MA: Cengage.

Ito, T. A., Larsen, J. T., & Cacioppo, J. T. (1998). Negative information weighs more heavily on the brain: the negativity bias in evaluative categorizations. *Journal of Personality and Social Psychology, 75*(4), 887–900.

Kassam, K. S., Morewedge, D. T., Gilbert, D. T. Wilson, T. D., & Wilson, T. D. (2011). Winners love winning and losers love money. *Psychological Science, 22*(5), 602-606.

Keast, R. S. & Costanzo, A. (2015). Is fat sixth taste primary? Evidence and implications. *Flavour, 4*(5). doi:1011862044724845.

Lawrence, J. J. (2008). Cholinergic control of GABA release: Emerging parallels between neocortex and hippocampus. *Trends in Neuroscience, 31*, 317 – 327.

Linden, D.J. (2015). Touch: *The Science of Hand, Heart and Mind.* Penguin Books.

McKeachie, W. J. (1986). *Teaching tips: A guidebook for the beginning college teacher.* Lexington, MA: D. C. Heath.

McKenzie. W. (2004). *A Hacker Manifesto.* Harvard University Press.

Merriam. S. B., & Clark, C. (2006). Learning from life experience: What makes it significant? *International Journal of Lifelong Education, 12*(2), 129–138. doi:10.1080/0260137930120205

Mezirow, J. (1990). How critical reflection triggers transformative learning. In J. Miller, G. (1956). The magical number seven, plus or minus two: Some limits on our capacity for processing information. *The Psychological Review, 63*, 81–97.

Pavlov, I. P. (1897). *The work of the digestive glands.* London, England: Griffin.

Perl, S. (2004). Felt sense: Writing with the body. Portsmouth, NH: Heinemann

Pink, D. H. (2005). *A whole new mind.* New York, NY: Penguin Books.

Pink, D. H. (2006). *A whole new mind.* New York, NY: Penguin Books.

Sanders, W. L., & Rivers, J. C. (1996). *Cumulative and residual effects of teachers on future student academic achievement.* Research Progress Report. Knoxville, TN: University of Tennessee Value-Added Research and Assessment Center.

Schutz, A. (1967). *Studies in social theory: Collected papers, II.* The Hague, Netherlands: Martinus Nijhoff.

Solms, M., & Turnbull, O. (2002). *The brain and the inner world.* London, England: Karnac.

Shook, J. (2014). What alerts, alters: Hacking the narratives of cultural memory with Rankine, Eady, and Philip. *Iowa Journal of Cultural Studies, 17*, 31–50.

St. Augustine. (n.d). *Confessions of St. Augustine.* Christian Classics Ethereal Library. Retrieved from https://www.ccel.org/ccel/augustine/confess.html

Toffolo, M. B., Smeets, M. A., & van den Hout, M. A. (2012). Proust revisited: Odours as triggers of aversive memories. *Cognitive Emotions, 26* (1), 83–92.

Wark, M. (2004). *A hackers manifesto.* Cambridge, MA: Harvard University Press.

Wheatley, M. Brainy quote. Retrieved from https://www.brainyquote.com/quotes/margaret_j_wheatley_283925

Yang, S. (2014). Wisdom and learning from important and meaningful life experiences. *Journal of Adult Development, 21*(3), 129–146. doi:10.1007/s10804-014-9186-x

www.ingramcontent.com/pod-product-compliance
Lightning Source LLC
Chambersburg PA
CBHW070944230426
43666CB00011B/2561